T0247773

Praise for *ChangeStories*

Change in organizations is actually simple in many ways, yet we make things incredibly hard for ourselves. A great deal has been written about change in organizations, much of which overcomplicates things or strays into vacuous thought leadership style pondering. In part this is because it evokes anxiety in clients and makes it easier to sell them 'solutions'. Susanne's book is different. It starts with a premise that might be best described as 'I think we might be overcomplicating things, folks, and here is what it would be useful to *actually* pay attention to'. Grounded in her experience as a change consultant working for large professional services firms, Susanne builds the case for how (re-) writing stories and narratives in organizations is at the heart of effective change. Crucially, she makes it clear that leaders need to build their capabilities in the area of storytelling and understand how change stands or falls on the tales people tell about their lived experiences – for good or ill. She is highlighting a key facet of the craft and practice of leading that is a million miles away from flashy, 'follow these steps', 'wield this model' approaches to change. Recommended.

Steve Hearsum
Founder, EDGE+STRETCH
Author of *No Silver Bullet: Bursting the Bubble of the Organisational Quick Fix*

The book is a story in itself – an easy and enjoyable read, providing the reader with the simple structure of the ARIAS model to follow, along with tips on how to build the learning into daily practice and links to supporting material. I really love the story-making template and have used this across change programmes and projects – its simplicity translates change into a clear, compelling and aligned message that is easy to understand and engage with. It transforms change from the language of project to the language of people. The template is now an essential in my change toolkit.

Rachel Butler
Head of Change, Anglian Water Services UK
Change Awards Winner of Best Capability Builder

This book is a fabulous read, a true wealth of resource, knowledge and wisdom that draws from Susanne's experiences and research. It's a true story in itself, bringing to life the power of stories to add value, interest and buy-in to any communication. For me, the difficulty is pulling out only one or two key themes, as I believe the entire book is important! The ARIAS model and storytelling template are so on-point and user-friendly, I can't wait to put these into practice. Whilst reading the book, I was already thinking about what areas of my work I could start to utilise these tools and techniques with.

Without people, successful change is impossible, and this book really teases out the importance of involving people whether they are senior leaders, change agents or employees on the ground. All stakeholders should be involved right from the start, and for those managing and leading the change, they must be able to win the hearts and minds of those impacted by the change. What also stuck with me was the authenticity of the storyteller and being your true self. There's no point telling a story if no-one's going to listen!

I would highly recommend this book for those wanting to try a different approach to building engagement and reinforcing change.

Joscelyn Henry-Shaw
PPM Profession Change Manager, NHS England

This is a very generous and appreciative piece of writing. Susanne writes as she works – in the deeply held belief that people in organizations can 'do' change with limited external support. In this book, she gifts to readers the practical set of tools that she uses in her change work with organizations. Susanne understands that we are meaning-making beings. With this in mind, she encourages us to notice the meaning we are making in the stories we tell and how we can use story to help others to do so.

There are many refreshing aspects of this book, not least Susanne's simple, practical and straight-talking language with her own stories. I read the book in three sittings – and having done so – can refer back when I need to to the many models and insights from her research of the literature, her practical experience with clients and her ChangeStories podcasts. I think Susanne hits the nail on the head when she writes about the need to pay attention to things as they are – with all our senses and ways of knowing, whilst giving heartfelt consideration to, 'what matters'. Most of all I enjoyed Susanne's candour in telling her own change story (which I know well), though I think if I told it, it would have more superlatives about her strengths as a colleague and change agent!

Ann Knights
Professor of Practice in Coaching and Leadership,
Hult International Business School
Co-author of *Relational Team Coaching*

A very honest and approachable way to get immersed into the world of change. It feels like you're getting advice from a friend all the way through, by someone giving you the inside scoop – I especially appreciated the practical questions and reflections throughout. If you're new to change or even a seasoned practitioner, there are excellent references, advice and approaches here that can really have an impact on how we think and bring change to life in our organisations.

Soraya Abdelmageed
Head of Change Management, Asahi Europe & International

Read Susanne Evans' book and like me, you'll want to immediately put her insights and principles into practice. With clear, captivating prose, organizational examples, helpful models and references (for more information) to her highly successful ChangeStories Podcast, Dr Evans leads us through the process of creating meaningful organizational change through storytelling. And in the process, she shifts our perspective on creating change: it's about the people not the process; change is messy and that's ok; be sure to welcome the disruptors and, especially, lead with appreciation. This book will become required reading for everyone experiencing change in their organization. And in these times, that is pretty much everyone!

Susanna Liller
PCC, President and Founder, The School for Real-Life Heroines
Author of *You Are a Heroine: A Retelling of the Hero's Journey*

Is it possible to love a book? I haven't in a long time read a book to the end, let alone read one that informed my practice. And then came *ChangeStories*, bringing me into the shared history of change that so many practitioners have to navigate. It instantly made my experiences feel seen. It made me switch off autopilot and dive into my own work and the stories in the changes around me. Storytelling in its own right is a tale as old as time, but what Susanne does in this book transcends fables and fairytales, positioning storytelling as an imperative to your change, its outcomes and your people. It shows wonderfully that there is another way to lead change, and it all starts with a good story. So yes, it's possible to love a book.

Susie Palmer-Trew
Founder, Everyday Change
Author of *The Everyday Change Playbook*

I first met Susanne at the beginning of her PhD and it has been such a pleasure watching her bring stories to life for organizations. In her wonderful book, her generosity of spirit shines through as she shares tools and her ARIAS model for coaches and organizations alike to use time and time again when their stakeholders need it most. Reading *ChangeStories* made me so happy as people not profit are at the centre of all she recommends as well as deeper inquiry to truly understand those around you. Having been an MD of a family business, I remember how our story kept us together as a strong team and set us apart from our competitors, but I didn't realise why until I read *ChangeStories*. I also learned first-hand as a coach and as an employee, what it feels like to be without the story during change, much like we felt during the uncertainty of Covid – vulnerable, unanchored, confused. Susanne's method and tools mean we can prevent this for future organizations.

Rebecca Mander
Executive Coach and Founder of GuruYou®

I find people tend to fall into one of two camps when it comes to the potential value of stories in change. Either 'storytelling is all fluff, and "once upon a time" has no place in a serious business,' or 'great, if I polish my story according to a proven model and make it shiny, everyone will love me and change will just happen.' Mmmm. Both are stories, and both are untrue. This book isn't about the idea of stories being an option in organizations. It reflects Susanne's deep appreciation of how people and organizations are already full of stories, which compete for our attention and with each other, and which need to be surfaced, heard and woven together if there is to be any real progress on any change. You can tell yourself you don't have time to read this book and reflect on your own use of stories. But that would be a story. Choose your stories wisely.

Alan Arnett
Thinking Partner and Coach, The Exploration Habit Ltd

In business, we often rely on PowerPoint presentations filled with facts and statistics. But let's be honest, while you're presenting, your audience is secretly planning their next coffee break. Even if you manage to persuade them, you've only convinced them intellectually. That's not enough to get people moving. Stories, on the other hand, grab people by the heart and mind, making them truly want to act. Susanne Evans' book is a powerful guide on how to use storytelling to drive change. It will transform the way you inspire and lead.

Andrea Pacini
Head of Ideas on Stage UK
Author of *Confident Presenter*

I very much enjoyed reading this book as I thought it not just gave the reader tools on how to manage and lead change, but it gave the reader a 'tell it how it is' with managing change. Susanne shares stories and case studies of previous experiences as well as the research and podcasts she has conducted within certain subject areas, giving you insight into her own journey of learning, discovering and helping others with change. There were several elements that really resonated with me, but to pick one, it would be the chapter on inquiry – I think change managers need to 'be curious, not judgemental' when working with clients to help uncover what is at the core of the organization. I also really liked the template Susanne shares on how to tell stories – I thought this was very practical and helpful for people to get started on sharing their own stories.

Jennifer Bryan
Founder and Managing Director of Leading Change
Vice President, Association of Change Management Professionals
Author of *Leading People in Change: A Practical Guide*

Storytelling has been a fundamental part of human history, and this incredibly practical book will help you harness its power to engage your audiences and unravel the mysteries of change. Susanne talks to you through the pages with practical and engaging insights, tools and techniques, signposting useful models and her own podcast episodes to allow you to delve into your own personal lightbulb moments. I cannot wait to use Susanne's storytelling template with some of my clients who are struggling to explain the *why* of change. Her comparison of individual reactions to change with responses to being asked to go swimming resonated deeply with me. Personally, I hate swimming, but my daughter loves it. The book teaches that this difference is precisely why we need to tap into everyone's personal perspective when asking them to embrace change. I love a book that helps me enhance my organizational development practice and makes me think, and this one does that in spades!

Kate Clarke
Founder, Kate Clarke Consulting Ltd

ChangeStories places storytelling at the heart of the change process, while reminding us that at heart, we are all storytellers. In our workplaces, communication often defaults to being formal and fact-based, and we favour pursuing a linear change progression over embracing its inherent messiness. Dr Susanne Evans makes a compelling case for leaders to involve people early and consider their real-world experiences during transitions. You will learn to embrace the mess, make genuine inquiries, have meaningful conversations and craft compelling stories. If you are sceptical of your own storytelling abilities, Susanne will reassure you as she wonderfully weaves her often humorous work–life stories throughout the book and provides practical tools to help you tell impactful tales.

Susan Ní Chríodáin
Facilitator and Coach
Author of *Leading Beyond the Numbers*
Host of Life Beyond the Numbers podcast

In my work, I'm surrounded by great storytellers who help people navigate through and make sense of the tumult of organizational changes. This book offers us a glimpse into what makes them so effective. Reading it has left me with greater confidence to find and tell more stories in my own work with change. A reminder of some of the most human – and often forgotten – practices of navigating workplace change, and a generous sharing of templates and structures to help you make your own stories to inspire action and engagement.

Through her own stories, Susanne reminds us how the stories that already exist in an organization can be coupled with new stories to create movement in the organization and build momentum from the old to the new, from the past through to the future. Not only a deeply helpful guide to finding, shaping and telling your own stories, but a timely reminder of some of the most human – and effective – ways of approaching change.

If I was leading a piece of organizational change, I'd want Susanne to be alongside me. And if that wasn't possible, I'd re-read this book.

Helena Clayton
Leadership Coach
Author of *Leading from Love*

ChangeStories podcasts have galvanised a community of passionate storytelling experts and here Susanne Evans brings this to life for leaders engaged in the messy business of change. The power of narrative to move the dial beyond strategic goals into organizational purpose and values is explained. Packed with insights, practical exercises and a new contribution with the ARIAS model, she advocates for leaders and followers working together to co-create change with a full understanding of their part in it. Key here is what matters to people, with reflection, attention and listening driving impactful change that reaches all corners of the business.

Vikki Kirby
Storytelling Research Fellow and Business Storytelling Advocate

A fascinating exploration into the origins, power and application of storytelling in everyday life. We all know how to tell stories. We do it with our friends all the time to build connection, to laugh and to reminisce. It is a tool that is frequently overlooked in organizational change and one we must try to lean on more. This book gives you the tools to create stories that can help you implement change more effectively, creating that same feeling of fun, joy and togetherness in your change initiatives. A crucial tool for all change leaders.

Ket Patel
Founder, Change Agitators
Change Management Institute Master Change Practitioner

ChangeStories reminds me of an Adam Grant or Malcolm Gladwell bestseller; it's non-fiction that is as compelling as a novel.

Susanne Evans combines fascinating stories with thought-provoking research, written in an accessible style. *ChangeStories* also includes practices and tools to help the reader apply the many ideas contained in the book.

Even though I've studied, practiced and taught storytelling for over 30 years, I repeatedly found myself surprised by, and appreciative of, the many new insights I gained from this book.

Whether you're simply interested in upping your general story-telling or game or specifically interested in using the power of storytelling to help people navigate change, this is a must-read.

David Lee
Founder of HumanNature@Work
Author of *Dealing with a Difficult Co-Worker*

Dr Susanne Evans

Change

Stories

How to have powerful conversations,
tell inspiring stories and build engagement
for transformation

First published in Great Britain by Practical Inspiration Publishing, 2024

© Susanne Evans, 2024

The moral rights of the author have been asserted

ISBN 978-1-78860-592-2 (hardback)
      978-1-78860-534-2 (paperback)
      978-1-78860-536-6 (epub)
      978-1-78860-535-9 (mobi)

Want to bulk-buy copies of this book for your team and colleagues? We can customize the content and co-brand *ChangeStories* to suit your business's needs.

Please email info@practicalinspiration.com for more details.

For Geraint, Mia and my whole family, whose continuous support makes everything possible

Contents

Foreword

Dr Angus Fletcher, Professor of Story Science, Project Narrative,
The Ohio State University

Stories are knowledge in action. Which is why another word for a story is a plot. And another word for a plot is a plan.

With a plan, we can transform ourselves and our world. And that transformation is story's biological purpose. Story evolved in the archaic brain to invent effective actions, and it remains core to human intelligence because it helped our ancestors imagine new futures that worked, evading threats and grasping opportunities.

If you want to solve problems, grow or innovate, there is no smarter or more powerful tool than story. Science shows: story is the maker of change.

Acknowledgements

I first had the idea of writing a book back in 2020, shortly after I had finished my PhD. So many people since then have supported and encouraged me through the process, probably too many people to mention here individually by name but hopefully you know who you are. My sincere thanks to everyone who has asked me how things are going, encouraged me when things have been difficult and allowed me to explore my ideas.

The greatest thanks go to my family and friends, who have patiently listened to me whilst I talked about change, storytelling and book writing. Your encouragement and support means so much to me and has made the writing process so much easier.

I am eternally grateful to everyone who took the time to meet with me whilst I was testing out my ideas for this book. I asked for volunteers to test out the templates and models and was overwhelmed by the response. Your ideas, suggestions and the discussions that we had have made this a better book.

Thank you to Alison Jones and the entire team at Practical Inspiration Publishing. You have looked after me every step of the way and it has been a real privilege to work with you, right from when I attended Alison's Book Proposal Challenge back in 2021 and this book started to take shape.

Huge thanks to Sam Warburton who created the illustrations for this book. I so enjoyed our discussions and love how you have captured what I wanted to express in this book through your work.

Thank you to everyone who has been a guest on the ChangeStories® podcast, who have shaped my own thinking about change and storytelling and whose insights feature in this book. Thank you too to everyone who listens to the podcast. I learn so much from the conversations that I have with my guests and it gives me so much joy to know that other people enjoy these conversations too.

Finally, thank you to everyone who continues to develop and expand the field of business storytelling. Since I first started learning about storytelling in 2008, I have come to see the power that stories have to create change and I feel immensely grateful to be part of the business storytelling community. Here's to the next chapter…

Introduction

More than 25 years ago, I embarked on my career as an organization change consultant, and heard stories about a large-scale change programme in a public sector organization. Unfortunately, the introduction of a new technology system was resulting in job losses and office closures. As a very junior consultant, my role was to support the more senior consultants in their work, as I learnt the basics of change management and how to use the tools and methods that the consultancy firm that I worked for used with their clients. I heard a war story from more experienced consultants who were sharing their experiences of working in the trenches of change with us newbies. This was probably done to scare us but also to prepare us for what was to come.

As a naive 20-something, I can remember being shocked at some of the behaviours that I heard about. Behaviours that at the time were considered to be the actions of employees who were being unreasonably resistant to a logical process of change. These behaviours went from a refusal to attend meetings to downright hostile and destructive actions, culminating with some employees blocking the sinks and toilets with toilet rolls and leaving the taps running as they left the building on their final day of employment.

At the time, I was shocked by these stories and sympathized with my colleagues who had borne the brunt of the actions of these employees. Over time, though, I heard more and more stories about how changes in organizations led to resistance, negativity and a battle between leadership and employees. And I became frustrated that none of the tools and methods that I had learnt seemed to offer any ideas for how to resolve this conflict and make change an easier process. In the business press, the drumbeat of change being a constant was increasing and yet there didn't seem to be any other way of creating change than what already existed. Frustrated with this, I left large-scale consultancy firms in 2007 and started my own company, hoping to find a different way.

A chance encounter in 2008 led me to the work of Robert McKee,[1] a Hollywood screenwriter, who shares his methods with leaders to enable them to communicate, persuade and influence using stories rather than conventional methods. I was introduced to his brilliant 2003 *Harvard Business Review* article 'Storytelling that Moves People' by Jon Harding, another consultant working with me on a piece of client work. On this project, a major change in the way that performance was managed in the organization was introduced using the principles of storytelling to build engagement. This contrasts with the conventional approach where, according to McKee:

… in the business world it usually consists of a PowerPoint slide presentation in which you say, 'Here is our company's biggest challenge, and here is what we need to do to prosper.' And you build your case by giving statistics and facts and authorities. But there are two problems with rhetoric. First, the people you are talking to have their own set of authorities, statistics and

experiences. While you are trying to persuade
them, they are arguing with you in their heads.
Second, if you do succeed in persuading them,
you've done so only on an intellectual basis.
That's not good enough, because people are not
inspired to act by reason alone.

Sounds familiar? It was certainly my experience of every change programme and leadership communication that I had ever experienced!

Reading this was like an explosion going off in my mind, blowing apart everything that I had previously learnt in my career but also explaining why sometimes creating change felt like pushing a boulder up a hill. On this project, I could already see the difference that taking a storytelling approach would have on the way that change could be embraced in an organization. I saw that leaders were more engaged in what was happening and were able to share their enthusiasm more authentically with their teams. I could see, hear and feel the buzz around this change which was different to any other project I had ever worked on. But at this stage I didn't really know why. The only thing that was different about this programme from others that I had worked on was that there was storytelling at the heart of the process.

I only worked on this project for six months, but it triggered something in me which meant I wanted to know more about the power of storytelling and to understand how to use it in my own practice. I also wanted to share this power with others in order for change to be less like a battle and more like a collaboration. This has been an ongoing process of learning and research, which continues to this day. Writing this book gives me an opportunity to share my own learnings since then, both from academic research and real-life stories of my experiences leading change:

Part I starts with an overview of why change can feel so difficult and explores ways to lead change differently that can overcome these difficulties, including why stories are important.

Part II explains the ChangeStories® ARIAS (Attention, Reflection, Inquiry, Appreciation, Storytelling) model which addresses head on the issues which are often forgotten about in change programmes and which can derail even the most well-executed change activity. Using this approach will enable you to increase engagement in change and enable employees at all levels, managers and leaders, to work together to create change, including having more meaningful conversations, telling inspiring stories and enabling genuine inquiry to create change that feels human and humane, and ultimately easier for everyone to get on board with.

Part III gives you the chance to build your own storytelling and performing skills with ideas about voice, visual and data storytelling, creating collaborative stories and much more.

Throughout, there are activities, reflective questions and links to episodes of the ChangeStories® podcast so that you can delve into the detail and take time to reflect on your own practice. I see reflection as a superpower in building change management and storytelling skills so you can use this book to guide you through this process. Please note that the podcast episodes suggested at the end of each chapter are as at time of writing. There are more episodes available online at www.changestories.co.uk

I'm really excited to share these insights with you as storytelling has transformed the way that I work and I know that it can do the same for you. Even adding a few elements of storytelling practice to your communications can make a huge difference.

Let's get started with some reflection about why change can feel really hard (and why it doesn't have to be).

PART I
CHANGE CAN BE DIFFICULT BUT IT DOESN'T HAVE TO BE

To begin, it's useful to take a step back and consider some of what we think we know about change and how sometimes this gets in our way. In this section:

▶ Chapter 1 considers what actually is a change and the history of change management in organizations, debunks some of the myths that have arisen about change management and uncovers some of the reasons why traditional methods of change management are doomed to fail.

▶ Chapter 2 asks the question 'how can change be led differently?' and offers some solutions to the issues uncovered in Chapter 1, including an introduction to the basic concepts of storytelling and why it is an important skill for everyone to learn.

Whilst I talk extensively about change management and change leadership in this book, I truly believe that actually everyone in an organization could (and should) be a change agent. So, whatever your current role in your organization, the skills in this book can add value to how you work on a day-to-day basis, as well as during periods of change.

Chapter 1
The history (and reality) of change management in organizations

It's a bit of a cliché but we are often told that change is difficult, and from personal experience I know that creating change in organizations can sometimes feel exhausting. Many people working in change management or people experiencing change in their organization feel the same.

To unpick why this is the case, it's useful to go right back to the beginning and try to understand what a change is and how change management as a specific job or a management activity came into being.

In this chapter, we will also consider some of the myths that surround change in organizations and why the more traditional way of managing change is bound to fail. There are links to specific ChangeStories® podcast episodes that discuss various elements of change management at the end of the chapter.

What is a change?

A change can take many forms and usually involves a change to the way that people work (process), a change to the tools that they use to work (technology) and/or a change to the number of employees (people). In large change programmes, all of these elements may be changed at the same time.

A change doesn't need to be particularly far reaching to have a big impact on how employees feel. Some of the most challenging changes that I have experienced have been about what might seem like minor things to management and leaders, such as staff uniforms, parking spaces and desk space. And yet, these have been difficult in terms of engagement with staff and willingness for people to get on board with the new way of doing things. Often this is because these are very personal and important to the individuals who are affected by it and this importance has been underestimated by the change team and/or leadership.

Since the 1940s, there has been a huge volume of literature (both academic and popular) related to the management of change in organizations. Much of the popular literature in this area has focused on providing tools and techniques for managers and change agents to use to manage change successfully in their own organizations. This literature assumes that change is something that can be successfully 'managed'. Even in the academic field, the focus on step-by-step guides for change is still evident.

These approaches often have a series of steps and activities which, if undertaken by a leader and/or a team of change agents, are assumed will lead to success. These change approaches have been taken up and used extensively by organization change consultants, both internal and external, as part of their tool kit. Whilst I am not going to review these approaches in detail here (there are plenty of other books available that do that), it is useful to consider how these approaches have evolved and shaped the practice and profession of change management today.

In their review of the literature of organization change, Rosenbaum, More and Steane[1] highlight the sheer volume of change models that have been developed since the mid-twentieth century, each of which have a number of differentiating factors. Models differentiate between types of change: whether change is planned or emergent, whether change is top down or bottom up and the size and impact of the change. In their paper, Rosenbaum, More and Steane argue that models of planned change focus either on governing change by providing 'specific approaches or steps that change agents and those who initiate change must address' (p. 289) or are structural in that they 'offer more of an overall framework within which change takes place' (ibid.).

Examples of these different approaches are summarized in the table below to illustrate the various aspects of these change models (adapted from Rosenbaum, More and Steane, 2018).

Model	Author	Key characteristics
Specific change steps (to be carried out in sequential order)		
Three-step model	Lewin (1947)	The original change approach which is directly linked to other planned organizational change approaches. Change is presented as a process of three stages – unfreezing the current state, creating a new state and then freezing the new state.

Model	Author	Key characteristics
Specific change steps (to be carried out in sequential order)		
7-S Model	McKinsey (1980)	This is one of the more complex models and, although the seven elements are not designed to be completed in a set order, they must all still be completed. The model includes: Hard elements – strategy, structure, systems Soft elements – styles, staff, skills, strategy The model is underpinned by shared values. There is an acknowledgement that the hard elements are simpler to identify and more easily controlled by management.
Eight-step model	Kotter (1996)	An evolution of Lewin where change is viewed as a project to be managed through a series of activities: Create a sense of urgency Build the change team Form a strategic vision Communicate the vision Remove barriers to change Focus on short-term wins Maintain momentum

Model	Author	Key characteristics
Specific change steps (to be carried out in sequential order)		
		Institute change
		Based on research in 100 organizations, this model led to the development of key lessons to be applied to other organizations experiencing change.
Framework within which change takes place		
Change curve	Kübler-Ross (1969)	Based on the experiences of grief, the change curve highlights the emotional reactions to change and gives ideas for responding to these:
		Denial
		Anger
		Bargaining
		Depression
		Acceptance
		A further evolution of Lewin's approach to include more focus on the human reactions to change.
Transitional-phase model	Bridges (1991)	A three-phase model with a particular focus on creating an end state and taking action to move to that point.

Model	Author	Key characteristics
Specific change steps (to be carried out in sequential order)		
		A further evolution to view change as a process of interpretation and sensemaking. This model will be discussed in more detail later in the chapter.
ADKAR	Hiatt (2003)	Linked to the Prosci consultancy firm, this is a bottom-up change model which is not sequential and was developed after studying change in over 700 organizations. Each letter represents a goal to be achieved in any change project: Awareness (of the need to change) Desire (to participate in and support the change) Knowledge (on how to change) Ability (to implement the necessary ways of working and behaviours) Reinforcement (to sustain the change)

Partly as a result of the development and use of these tools, the role of the change management consultant grew extensively as a profession in its own right in the latter part of the twentieth century. This is the environment in which I first encountered change management and still forms the basis for how change is managed in many organizations today.

Alongside the limitations of these existing models of change, we are also told that change is difficult and likely to fail. This is a key myth about change which I am keen to debunk here.

Debunking the change management myths

You may have heard the statistic that 70% of change fails and this may fill you with fear about any future changes that you may be involved in. You may have read other books and articles that emphasize the difficulty of creating change, all of which make you nervous. It doesn't have to be this way.

Firstly, the statistic that 70% of change fails is flawed and now largely discredited, particularly through the work of Dr Mark Hughes.[2] The 70% statistic was misquoted from the original article title in the *Harvard Business Review*[3] which, if you read it, offers a much more subtle and nuanced analysis of change failure. (If you are interested in finding out more about Dr Mark Hughes' debunking of this myth, listen to episode 26 of the ChangeStories® podcast where we have an in-depth discussion about it and links to Mark's research papers are included in the show notes. You can find all the podcast episodes at www.changestories.co.uk)

These narratives of change failure started to circulate when there was also a shift from managing change to leading change and also at a time when business schools and consultancies had a vested interest in making change seem difficult. The truth is that 'success' as a concept in change is difficult to measure as so much of it is in the eye of the beholder. What success looks and feels like to a leader in an organization may be different to what success looks and feels like to an employee or a shareholder. Also, existing research into organization change success examines organizations at a specific moment in time, rather than measuring the outcomes of change (good or bad) over a period of time.

But even though we now know that the statement that 70% of change fails is untrue, it can still feel difficult to achieve what we want from a change programme. Often, these difficulties are down to issues with communication of the change and the subsequent engagement with it by employees. There is often also an assumption that people intrinsically dislike change, another myth that is simply not true.

People are better at dealing with change than they (and we as change practitioners and leaders) think they are. Consider the Covid pandemic and how quickly organizations and individuals responded to the change and quickly changed everything about the way that they worked. It was a very challenging situation but people responded to it. This shows that we can change when we need and want to.

The problem is that some of the more 'traditional' ways of managing and leading change contribute to this myth of change being difficult. Some of this is because there has been a desire to portray change as difficult so that organizations need help in managing it and therefore employ consultants to do this for them. (I recognize the irony of me writing this as an organization change consultant but also feel strongly that organizations should be able to manage change themselves without as much reliance on external help.) The excellent book by Steve Hearsum, *No Silver Bullet*, provides a brilliant analysis of the evolution of the role of the management consultant and the inherent tension between managers and leaders wanting a quick fix for organizational issues (which do not exist) and the willingness of consultants to provide these solutions. I'll return to this point shortly.

In addition, the existing organization change tools (as described earlier in this chapter) are, on their own, not fit for purpose and do not focus on what is important during periods of change. This can make us feel like these tools are not working for us or that we are not using them properly or are failing in our change efforts. In fact, they don't work because they do not address some of the fundamental forces that exist in organizations, for example:

> ▶ Taking too much of a process focus to change can result in a lack of focus on people;

> ▶ Organizations often approach change as an exercise that can be 'sheep dipped' to everyone without taking account of individual needs. In reality, change is a lot messier than this;

> ▶ Little account is taken of the past within the organization which can shape how change is managed in the future.

Let's examine each of these in turn.

Too much focus on process

Many changes in organizations are managed as part of a large transformation programme which often comes with project management processes built in. This can lead to a change being approached as a series of steps which, if completed, will ultimately lead to success. After all, this is the model of change which most of us are familiar with and this was certainly my experience when I worked in large consultancy firms supporting organizations to create change.

Whilst it is important to manage projects and programmes with care to ensure that they run to time and budget, too much focus on the process can lead to a lack of focus on the people, the employees, who ultimately will drive the change. And because people are individuals, they will have different reactions and approaches to change, which may or may not support the timescale and activities of a project plan. A more people-focused approach to change is needed, and this is where storytelling and conversation come into the mix. I'm not saying that you need to replace project management methodologies with this approach; they can run alongside to make a change programme that really works for the people in the organization.

Change professionals and leaders in organizations are often attracted to linear, process-driven models of change as they appear to give us control over change and the answers that we want to make change easier. Steve Hearsum[4] talks about the desire for a 'silver bullet' to make change easy – which simply doesn't exist as there is no single answer. This links back to the previous discussion about the motivation for external change consultants and business schools to make change seem difficult. By presenting themselves as the silver bullet to make change easy, these individuals and organizations are also prescribing themselves as the cure. This creates an unbalanced relationship between the client and the consultant where the consultant is the saviour and the client the victim, which can lead to dependency and bad practice. The fact is, change is messy (as we will see in the next section) and it is a mistake to try and manage it simply as a programme that follows a set of logical steps.

As a leader and/or a change agent, it can be scary to accept the messiness of change and relinquish control from this aspect of a change programme. However, approaching change with the mindset that it won't necessarily follow your neat and tidy project plan can help. Yes, use the project plan as a guide but also be prepared to be flexible in approach to respond to issues that might occur.

The suggestions in this book will help with this as it will allow you to learn more about how people are feeling in the organization about the change and respond accordingly. One of the key questions that I like to ask when I'm working in organizations is 'what do you need?', and then respond. This approach enables me to focus on what will actually make a difference rather than sticking rigorously to a methodology. This is not a simple solution to why change can feel difficult, however. But, it does give you an opportunity to add other tools such as storytelling to your change management toolbox and to experiment, listen, engage and learn – something that is missing from the more traditional approaches to change management. There is no reason that you can't build this approach into your project plan, it just needs to be factored in.

Change is individual and messy

I often think about swimming as a metaphor for how people feel about change. I love to swim. But, for many people, swimming or being underwater is a frightening experience. Many of us, even the most confident swimmers, will remember the scary feeling of having to go to the deep end of the pool for the first time. Being out of your depth can be very unnerving.

On one of my recent trips to the pool, I saw a group of young children heading to the deep end for the first time with their swimming teacher. Some of them jumped right in and some needed some help. And some refused to do it altogether. It reminded me of the different reactions that people have to organization change.

Organizations and teams are made up of individuals, all of whom will have their own preferences for communication and engagement. Whilst it would be extremely difficult and time-consuming to create an individualized change programme for each employee, an element of individualized content and approach is helpful in truly supporting people through change.

Change in organizations can be complicated. But, if more time is taken to understand individuals rather than treating everyone the same, change will be more sustainable. After all, you can't change an organization, you can only change the people within it. Be like the swimming teacher, allowing employees to change at their own rate and take the plunge when they are ready.

On one of the most successful change programmes that I worked on, we created a set of materials and content about the change which line managers then adapted to use in their team meetings, using the internal training team and members of the change programme to facilitate as required. This enabled a more tailored approach without having to create separate content for every person, but still enabled the content and approach to feel tailored to the individual. We then took questions at the end of each meeting and responded to those next time. Much like the question 'what do you need?' mentioned above, this approach enabled us to really understand people's individual needs rather than sheep-dipping them through some change management training.

Talking about change management training, many organizations continue to refer to the Change Curve, developed by Elizabeth Kübler-Ross[5] (and which is summarized earlier in this chapter) as their benchmark for supporting people through change. This model was originally developed as a way to illustrate the phases of grief that people go through when they lose a loved one or experience trauma and, personally, I think that it offers some useful words to describe how people might feel during a period of change. But that is all. The idea that every person in every organization will feel the same during every change and follow a linear trajectory through their feelings is not representative of my own experiences of working with people going through change. I also think that, along with the language of change failure discussed earlier, associating a change with death through the change curve is a major factor in why change is so often perceived negatively and with trepidation by leaders and employees alike.

In my PhD research, I discovered that over a period of three years, the individuals that I worked with experienced a whole range of feelings, moving backwards and forwards from supporting the change, to being against the change and back again. They certainly didn't move smoothly from one end of the change curve to the other. Individual reactions to change can be based on a variety of different factors including personal preferences, previous experiences of change and willingness to tolerate uncertainty and ambiguity. I prefer to think of reactions to change as more of a knotted ball of string rather than a linear curve. This messy version of the change curve shows that, in the end, most people end up in the right place, but there might be a bit of a difficult patch in the middle:

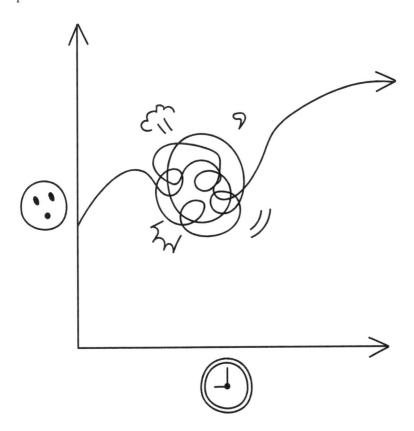

Change can be messy but that is because it involves people, in all of their messy, emotional glory, and we need to recognize that in the way that we approach change. Tom Harford has developed the messy theme further in his book.[6] Here, he argues that messiness is essential for creativity, ideas and new thinking. Whilst he does not suggest that disruption is always a good thing, he does suggest that being too rigid in our thinking can be disempowering and constraining. He recommends that we discard rules and rigidity and embrace the creativity that can emerge when we accept the messiness of everyday life. He argues that the greatest and most difficult changes that we face can be the most transformative. Thinking about change as a messy experience can help us to feel better about it (and our ability to manage it) when things aren't going our way. And it can also help us to be more creative and innovative when we are not trapped by linear thinking.

Accept that change is messy and that there is no straight path to the other side. Embrace the messy and the opportunities that it brings. Acknowledge and accept all of the feelings, good and bad, that you might have in relation to change. They are all OK. And progress through a change at your own rate, rather than feeling like you have to conform to a model.

One model of change that I think is far better at representing the reality of change for people is Bridges' transition model,[7] which is summarized earlier in this chapter. Bridges characterizes a change as an external event or situation that takes place and the transition is the inner psychological process that people go through as they come to terms with the new situation. This is a helpful distinction as it enables us to think about change as an ongoing process rather than a one-off exercise. For example, when we move house, the change is the move, the transition is all the stuff that has to happen later such as finding new schools, a new doctor or dentist and changing our address with the bank etc. So, a change will only be successful if leaders and organizations address the transition that people experience through change.

In Bridges' model, there are three stages, beginning with an ending. Yes, ending is the starting point of a change, which seems paradoxical but is true. The first phase of a transition begins when people identify what they are losing and learn how to manage these losses. They determine what is over and what they will keep. This could include relationships, processes, team members or places of work. This is followed by the neutral zone when people go through an in-between time when the old is gone but the new isn't fully operational. It is when the critical psychological realignments take place and is the very core of the transition process. People are creating new processes and learning what their new role will be. They are in a state of flux and may feel confusion or distress. But this is the start of a new beginning. New beginnings are often marked by a release of energy in the new direction and a realization of a new identity. Well-managed transitions allow people to establish new roles with an understanding of how to contribute and participate most effectively. And as a result, they feel more engaged with the organization and its purpose.

It's useful to identify these endings and beginnings and you can work through the Bridges model either on your own or with a group to reflect on any change that is taking place in your organization.

Activity – The Bridges Transition Model

You should allow 30 minutes for this exercise. You will need pens, Post-it notes (two different colours) and flipcharts or you can facilitate this remotely using Teams whiteboards (or similar). If you are running this activity with a group, briefly explain the Transition model first before commencing the activity. You can also use this as a thinking exercise to complete on your own.

Whether you are completing this on your own or in a team:

- Think about (and discuss if in a group) the changes that are happening within the organization

- Write down or share the things that need to be let go of. Stick these on a flipchart titled 'Letting Go'

- Using a different colour of Post-it note, write down things that you want to hold on to. Stick these on a flipchart titled 'Holding On'

- Review the outputs and then consider what this means for the success of the change

Just as our own experiences from the past are different, and these will shape our future reactions (more on this later), we are also all wired differently. Much has been written about the neuroscience of organization change and I will return to an approach that I particularly like later in this book, the SCARF model by David Rock.[8] Feeling uncertain is a fairly common feeling during change. In psychological terms, uncertainty is a state which is caused by an individual's perception of the environment that they find themselves in. This perception can cause people to feel differently about uncertainty. For some, uncertainty creates excitement and opportunities to try new things, make mistakes and learn from them. For others, uncertainty can cause stress and psychological strain. As David Rock discusses, this can lead to a fight or flight response in the brain which can limit performance and creativity.

In my view, we can all flip from one side of the scale to the other. Sometimes, we will find uncertainty difficult to deal with and at other times we won't. This can be due to the situation that we find ourselves in, our motivations and our emotions on a particular day. Because we are dynamic and we don't react the same way all of the time. A key factor in the amount of stress that an individual will feel in relation to an uncertain situation is the level of control that they feel over it. A feeling of loss of control can lead to an increase in psychological strain, particularly if this is accompanied by feelings of uncertainty about how the change will progress and what the outcomes will be. Most importantly, having opportunities to participate in and find solutions makes the most difference to employee feelings of stress caused by change.[9] There is more on this later in the book.

History matters

The history of the organization and the impact that this can have on the sustainability of change within an organization cannot be underestimated. The shared history of an organization is what binds people together and creates a clear sense of what it means to be in an organization and what behaviours are acceptable. In relation to change, this could be the way in which change has been introduced and led in the past and could also be the actual history of the organization itself. And, of course, each individual in the organization will also have their own history within (and outside) of the organization.

These factors can act as anchors that ground an organization and the individuals within it in the present rather than enabling changes to be enacted in the future. I'll illustrate this with a story that I heard in an organization that I worked with some time ago.

This organization had been in existence for over 100 years and in that time had changed very little, other than with the introduction of some new technology. Unfortunately, it had become necessary to make some redundancies and close some offices down, the first time that this had happened in the history of the organization. The change team had carefully planned to undertake the change slowly, recognizing that the pace of change had been slow in the past in the organization and so change could only be achieved at this pace. So, people who were being made redundant were given over 12 months' notice so that they could find another job at their own pace. During this time, the office remained open and support was given to them as they tried to find work.

So far, so good – a very human-centred approach to change.

However, during this 12-month period, life carried on as usual in the office. Christmas came, decorations were put up and then packed away under the stairs, ready to donate to a local charity when the office closed. The person who had volunteered to donate the decorations left and the decorations were forgotten about. But, because they were still under the stairs, the story started to circulate that the office wasn't in fact closing and was going to remain open. Because the decorations were where they always had been, and therefore would be going up again in December.

Of course, when the time came to finally give the remaining employees notice that the office would be closing in a month, it was a shock to people. There was anger and upset because the dominant force in this organization was for things to continue as they always had done. By failing to recognize all the elements of what it meant to work in this organization, the change leaders missed one of the most important aspects – that the past can feel very comfortable to people and, sometimes, there is an unwillingness to move forward. And people can attribute facts to objects and artefacts that reinforce this history. To compound this further, the leadership and change team in this organization either didn't hear or didn't pay any attention to the stories that were circulating about the Christmas decorations.

In this case, it wasn't about the Christmas decorations. It was actually about the past history of change (or lack of it) that convinced people that, actually, this planned change wasn't going to happen. And the Christmas decorations under the stairs just reinforced this view.

Therefore, attention needs to be paid to this history before change is begun to understand what is actually achievable in this organization. I referred earlier to previous experiences of change being a factor that influences how people deal with change in the future. This is true at an individual and at an organizational level. To create successful change, there needs to be a period of reflection and inquiry at the start of the process to think about what changes have taken place in the past and what lessons can be learnt from them. This reflection and inquiry period, which will be discussed in more detail later in the book, enables leaders and change practitioners to understand the hidden factors in any organization, such as the history of change, which can act as anchors and barriers to change.

Memories and stories about the past in the organization and nostalgia about what the organization used to be like and what the values of the organization used to be can be very powerful. I heard a story from a client a few weeks ago where there were some very compelling stories circulating about what the organization used to be like and how much better it had been in the past. It emerged that the people telling these stories had not even witnessed the incidents that they described. But the stories were still being told as examples of how the organization had changed, for the worse!

As well as history and memories in organizations, much of what happens in organizations takes place below the surface, just like an iceberg. Some of these factors can also act as a barrier or an enabler to change. Edgar Schein's culture model[10] is a good illustration of these factors. Schein's model includes a number of factors, some of which are easy to see and understand and some of which are hidden and require effort to uncover:

- Organizational artefacts – tangible processes and structures, easy to gather but hard to interpret

- Espoused values – strategies, goals, vision and values

- Underlying assumptions – unconscious beliefs, taken for granted assumptions, ultimate source of action

These underlying assumptions are hard to see and understand if you only take a surface view of what is going in the organization, i.e. what you can actually see. However, these can have a major impact on how effective change can be implemented in an organization. It is important to surface and understand cultural factors and stories about the past so that we know what we are up against when we are trying to enact change. In addition, people are more likely to change if something from the past that they value continues, so having this knowledge can help us. Employees are also more likely to accept a change if they feel that it fits with their values or the values of the organization, as they see them. Past experiences will also shape how employees perceive any future change activities.

Because of their previous experiences of change, some employees will view change as dangerous whilst others will perceive it as something exciting. In many existing approaches to organization change, employee views on change are not gathered or analysed to determine how this might impact on the change programme. In an interesting study in 2017, Rafferty and Restubog[11] discovered that 'when employees report that previous change efforts in that company have not been successful and have been poorly managed, they are less likely to report that current changes present an opportunity for growth' (p. 541). This finding was even greater for older employees or those with a long period of service with the company. This will come as no surprise to anyone who has tried to introduce anything new in an organization, particularly a new piece of technology. When I have been working on these projects, I constantly hear stories starting with 'well, last time we did this...' before hearing how everything went wrong last time. This can be challenging to deal with without listening to these stories and then making efforts to ensure that things happen differently on the next project.

In his study of change in the NHS, Mervyn Conroy[12] identified how important it is for leaders to understand the real world of people experiencing change, in order for the change to be successful. He critiqued existing organizational theory as being 'structural functional in nature... a set of qualitative factors or models of change that offer a guide to practitioners of what "levers" to focus their attention on. The belief is that by pulling or pushing on these levers, change can be controlled and stable outcomes predicted' (p. 236). He argues that it is essential to understand narratives as part of change in order to identify how the purpose and values of the organization are created and developed.

You might be thinking at this point that this feels like a lot of extra work for the change leader or change agent and wondering how you build all of this into your practice. This book is here to help you answer this question. By changing the way that change is communicated and planned and building in story, inquiry and conversation, a greater likelihood of success is achieved. And this has led me to develop the ChangeStories® ARIAS model to support organizations in doing this. We will examine this in detail in Part II of this book.

In the meantime, if you want to find out more about change management practice and learn some lessons from other practitioners in the field, there are a number of episodes of the ChangeStories® podcast that focus on this:

- ▶ Episode 16 – Alan Arnett. Confessions of a change practitioner.

- ▶ Episode 24 – Jude Jennison. Becoming more comfortable with uncertainty.

- ▶ Episode 26 – Dr Mark Hughes. The strange (but true) story of change failure.

- ▶ Episode 34 – Ket Patel. What is change management anyway and do we even need it?

- ▶ Episode 40 – Melanie Franklin. Measuring and building change capability.

- ▶ Episode 42 – Mark Green. Putting the fun back into change management.

Chapter 2
Leading change differently using stories

Before I go on, I do want to say that this book is not here to rubbish other tools and models of change. Many of them do have their place and the ChangeStories® ARIAS model can be used alongside any of them to enhance the way that change is managed in any organization. However, recent research into change leadership in the twenty-first century suggests that there are a variety of skills that are now needed to create successful change:[1]

- ▹ Open and honest engagement;

- ▹ Authenticity about your own fears and those of others;

- ▹ Willingness to live without consensus for a while;

- ▹ Changing yourself, not just asking others to change;

- ▹ Having courageous conversations about change;

- ▹ Setting realistic expectations about what can be achieved;

▶ Enlisting people in the change and keeping them committed;

▶ Being the engine of change, not just managing or minimizing it;

▶ Creating a big vision (who we are and where are we going?) and empowering people;

▶ Being resilient in the face of ambiguity;

▶ Accepting that things might feel a little bit out of control at times;

▶ Examining your own way of operating and making changes.

Many of these factors are simply not included in existing change practice and so, to create this sort of change environment, a focus on leading change in a different way is required, and to do this there are a few basics that need to be in place from the beginning:

▶ Involve people early and throughout;

▶ Understand what is important to people;

▶ Tell a compelling story about the change.

This book is structured to build your confidence and skills in key areas to address these basic building blocks of change – building inquiry and conversation into change practice, uncovering the hidden factors that can hinder change in organizations and using storytelling skills to create engaging communications and narratives about change. These skills will give you the power to create better change in your organization.

These elements are brought together in the ChangeStories® ARIAS model that will support you in building your storytelling skills and using them in your everyday practice.

Involve people early and throughout

Change cannot be top down. Employees must be included throughout the change process. And this shouldn't just be communication. It needs to be full involvement, with employees being given the opportunity to share their stories and experiences of change and ask questions throughout the change process. These stories should then be used to shape the way that change is enacted.

Having conversations and asking questions is a way of dealing with the messiness of change *and* improving engagement in change. I've noticed on many of the change projects that I have worked on that where a change is creating anxiety for employees, it stifles conversation at precisely the time when conversation is most needed. As a leader or change practitioner, it is so important to create an environment where conversation is both enabled and encouraged.

A common (and very human) reaction of some leaders during times of uncertainty is to reduce their visibility. For many leaders, not knowing the answer can feel very uncomfortable, leading to them hiding away or speaking from a script. Actually, during times of change and uncertainty, it's even more important for leaders to show up and be visible. To put themselves out there and be prepared for the awkward questions. And admit when they don't know the answer.

I heard a story from a colleague recently who had asked participants on a training course to recall examples of strong and authentic leadership from their past careers. One individual shared a story that had happened some time before but which had stuck with him because it was so powerful. He told a story about a new leader starting work in the organization and inviting everyone to meet with him at a large-scale meeting where everyone could ask whatever questions they wanted. There was no preparation or pre-submission of questions as had been the case at similar events in the past. At this event, a number of questions were asked which the new leader clearly didn't know how to answer. Rather than waffling or avoiding the question, the leader said that he didn't know the answer but that he would take the question away and then get back to people with the answer once he knew more. And a few days later, he did. This was such a stark contrast to previous management practice that immediately people realized that the experience of working for this individual would be different. The experience was a powerful illustration of authentic and open leadership and showed the employees that things were going to change.

For leaders, it's also important to create a sense of purpose for others. Storytelling is a great tool for this. Linking back to engaging employees in solution finding, engaging employees in co-creating a story has been shown to be very valuable in creating positive outcomes during change.[2]

Understand what is important to people

Consideration needs to be given to the way that employees perceive themselves within the organization. So often, individuals are characterized as change champions or as resistant to change by others. Actually, what is most important is how people see themselves. Again, this can be understood through the stories that people tell about change and how they see themselves within it. And this information can then be used to shape change activity so that is less scary.

In the past when I worked on change projects, I would undertake a stakeholder analysis at the beginning of the project and use this to plan how I interacted with and communicated with these stakeholders throughout. My research showed, however, that stakeholders' views changed throughout the three years that I worked with them, and so it is important to be more iterative in our assessments.

I discovered that employees' views about how they saw themselves in relation to the change was very dynamic. One month they supported the change, then they didn't and felt connected to people that they had previously seen as resisters, then they liked the external consultants who were brought in to lead the project. And then they disliked the consultants! All of this adds to the complexity of change, which is often not recognized in change programmes.

So, go back to basics. Check in with people to see what they need. Understand what the change means to different individuals and teams and the impact that it will have on them. Consider what is important to people about the organization in the past and present and how this can be carried forward into the future. At the very least, understand 'what is in this change for me?' for the various stakeholders in your organization. And then use all of this information as you talk to people about the change to create a compelling story.

Storytelling is at the heart of this approach. Both as an essential tool to shape communications and also as a way to listen to and understand what is going on within organizations. I continue to be amazed at the difference that building elements of storytelling practice in to change activities can make. So, before we go any further, here are some story basics.

Tell the story

Many managers and leaders struggle to articulate a clear vision of the change and what the future will look like and then find it difficult to share this future vision with others. This is where storytelling can really play a part, enabling the creation of a meaningful and personal story of the future so that everyone can understand what their future in the organization will look and feel like. This is not about making a story up about the future. It's about finding and making use of information that already exists in the organization and then crafting it into an engaging change story.

This is different from many change communications which are focused at the strategic level and/or the activities that the change team are working on. This approach really focuses on what is in the change for every person in the organization and paints a picture of this future in real and concrete terms.

Adorisio[3] provides us with a simple definition of a story as '... someone tells someone else something has happened...' The key emphasis of this definition is the social interaction, i.e. that to be a story one individual has to tell another individual something. This definition is echoed by Norman Denzin, who writes:[4]

A story is an account involving the narration of a series of events in a plotted sequence which unfolds in time. A story has a beginning, a middle and an ending. Stories have certain basic structural features, including narrators, plots, setting, characters, crises and resolutions.

We will examine these features in more detail later in this chapter and throughout this book.

Stories are a powerful way to communicate and engage during a period of change – actually, for any form of communication at any time. There are a number of reasons for this, which are explored in more detail below:

- ▷ Humans are hard wired to love stories, from childhood;

- ▷ Stories are sense-making experiences, particularly during periods of uncertainty;

- ▷ Stories create emotion and action.

Humans are hard wired to love stories, from childhood

Just think about your earliest memories and many of them will be associated with listening to stories, reading stories or using your imagination. That is certainly my experience. I can remember walking home from school when I was very young and making up a story about the walk, sometimes based on the characters in a television show (Heidi was a particular favourite for me from the 1980s) and sometimes just based on my imagination. Most of us will have had similar experiences as children.

People have told stories for more than 20,000 years, initially using visual forms such as cave paintings to share experiences and keep each other safe. Then stories became oral and can be found in myths, plays, art and, in more modern times, written forms and on television. These early stories helped to transmit information about what behaviours were acceptable and prepare for the future, and thus it has been argued that stories have been essential for human evolution and survival. There is some evidence that oral storytelling was a key part of the early human experience. For example, many cultures share similar stories and myths about floods and this has led some researchers to conclude that these stories can be directly traced back to oral stories told at the end of the last ice age, around 10,000 years ago. I find that longevity of story incredible. Imagine harnessing some of that storytelling power in your own practice!

Yang, in his article 'Telling Tales at Work' (2013) argues that the early humans needed to use stories to understand their environment and this increased the rate in which language was developed. He argues that the evolution of language improved the chances of survival if it enabled our early ancestors to communicate threats effectively. Stories are better at doing this than simple gestures and the better storytellers were more likely to have a stronger chance of survival:

> ... elaborate storytelling must have emerged
> as an adapted cognitive device for collecting
> and sharing important social and geographical
> information, which was critical for our foraging
> ancestors in terms of the successful exploitation
> of scattered resources. (p. 135)

Humans are naturally interested in stories as we are social creatures and research has shown how stories create neurological reactions in the brain. In his article in the *Harvard Business Review*, Paul Zak[5] showed that subjects produced the stress hormone, cortisol, during tense moments in a story and a story with a happy ending led to a release of dopamine, resulting in feelings of happiness. This reaction may explain, in part, why we are drawn to stories.

Stories as sense-making experiences

I was asked recently about things that I found particularly inspiring or that created emotion. When I considered this, I thought about an artwork that I had recently seen that took my breath away. I was lucky enough to visit the Apocalypse Tapestries at Angers Chateau in the autumn of 2023 and the size, scale and antiquity of the tapestries were incredible. But when asked to recall any facts about them, all I could tell you (without referring to Google) would be that they were made for someone important in about the thirteenth century. What did stick with me, though, was the story of how the tapestries had been forgotten about in the eighteenth century, cut up and used on a farm to fix holes in barn walls and insulate orange trees and how they were then rediscovered in the early twentieth century. The key facts about the artwork had been lost to me but the story had stuck around and actually was probably the thing that I found most amazing about the tapestries.

An interesting experiment, called Significant Objects,[6] was carried out in 2009 where objects were bought at thrift stores for a few dollars. A writer would invent a story about the object which was then sold on eBay, with the story as the only description of the object. (It was made clear in the description that this story had been written by a professional writer so that the purchaser was in on the experiment.) The theory (by the authors of the study, Joshua Glenn and Rob Walker) was that the story would increase the perceived value of the object and thus it would sell for a higher price. As Glenn and Walker stated: 'Stories are such a powerful driver of emotional value that their effect on any given object's subjective value can actually be measured objectively.'

The result of this experiment was that $128.74 of thrift store junk was sold for $3,612.51, with this uplift attributed to the story that accompanied the object. I love this experiment and the story behind it. For me it really illustrates the power of a story to add value to any object but also to add power and interest to communications.

Research conducted by Stephens, Silbert and Hasson in 2010[7] found that people listening to life stories had very strong reactions in specific parts of the brain in response to the story. In fact, the activity in the listener's brain mirrored that of the storyteller. This mirroring did not happen when the listeners were only told a series of facts. Echoing the work of Zak, the researchers suggest that this mirroring is why stories are such effective methods of communication as they trigger parts of the brain linked to feelings and emotions. This mirroring reaction is also essential in enabling us to understand other people's point of view.

So, stories are part of our every day life and are a natural way for us to remember and share information and to make sense of complex and uncertain situations. Outside the workplace, most of our communication is story based and yet this is not repeated in work. Think about the last time you met up with your friends or family. I bet that most of the communication that you did with them was telling stories about things that had happened to you since you saw them last. Or even stories that they have been told before but that are entertaining and make you all laugh. But what happens when we are in the workplace? We forget this natural storytelling ability that we all have and revert to a different form of communication that is much more formal and fact based.

It's difficult to know exactly why this is but I think it is because we see non-story-based forms of communication all around us when we enter an organization, and so over time we too start using this form, even if it doesn't come naturally to us. This is seen as the accepted form of business communication. But the tide is changing and there is greater recognition all the time about how storytelling is a natural communication form for all of us and is appropriate for use in the workplace. We all love stories but somehow forget this when we are at work. Well, now is the time for this to change!

A great example of how we use stories to make sense of the world around us is the Heider and Simmel illusion. I have shown this film to many different people over the years and it is really interesting to see the different interpretations of the shapes moving around on the screen.

Activity – The Heider and Simmel Illusion

Watch the clip now (go to www.youtube.com/watch?v= 8FIEZXMUM2I) before moving on. Note what you saw and what you were thinking about when you watched it.

What did you think about? Nine out of ten people tell a story when they watch this film of random shapes, so if you created a story, you are not alone. As David Eagleman says in *The Brain – The Story of You*:

> When people watched this short film and were asked to describe what they saw, you might expect that they described simple shapes moving around. After all, it's just a circle and two triangles changing coordinates. But that's not what the viewers reported. They described a love story, a fight, a chase, a victory. Heider and Simmel used this animation to demonstrate how readily we perceive social intention all around us. Moving shapes hit your eyes, but we see meaning and motives and emotion, all in the form of a social narrative. We can't help but impose stories. From time immemorial, people have watched the flight of birds, the movement of stars, the swaying of trees, and invented stories about them, interpreting them as having intention. This kind of storytelling… unmasks the degree to which our brains are primed for social interaction.

What does this tell us?

That people use stories a lot to explain things when they are uncertain of what they are seeing.

What does this mean for us during a period of change?

If people are already thinking in stories, then it makes sense to use stories to communicate about change but also listen to stories that you hear that might be telling you about how people feel about the change.

Stories are important ways of meaning and sense-making for us and by using them in how we talk about change we can paint a picture of the future. Scott McArthur described this as describing 'the edge of next' when we talked about storytelling in a podcast episode. He described storytelling as a way to enable people to explore the future, use their imagination to discover the art of the possible and prepare and recover from change. As Angus Fletcher said to me in our conversation, 'every day is a possibility to discover a new story.'

Stories create emotion and action

A story should include:

- An audience for the story, whether it is verbal or written, and a storyteller or narrator;

- A setting which is explained at the beginning at the story;

- A set of characters with human or human-like characteristics;

- A plot including a series of causal actions and consequences often in the form of a number of sequential episodes and the building of suspense until the eventual resolution of any conflicts or crises. These conflicts or crises are seen to be critical parts of a story, with the protagonist's efforts to overcome adversity being essential;

▷ A sequential telling (i.e. with a beginning, a middle and an end) of the conflict or crises and the eventual resolution. This is what makes a story meaningful in its entirety. In addition, the causality between events in the story, which can be either implied or explicit, is what makes stories different from other sequential accounts. Stories are situated in time or space;

▷ The outcome of the story is that the audience feels some emotion and/or connection to the story characters.

It is this final point that makes a story different from simply a list of things that happened, like reading out the entries in someone's diary. It is the causal structure with a protagonist and an end goal that truly engages the listener or reader of a story. Without this, simply hearing about something that happens to someone else would not be interesting. As Lisa Cron[8] explains, it can't just be hearing about someone else that is interesting to us '... otherwise we'd be utterly enthralled reading a stranger's... journal chronicling every trip she took to the grocery store ever – and we're not!'

It is interesting to note (and we will return to story structures in more detail later in the book) how consistent this structure is in stories from across the world and from different time periods. It's not a universal formula but it does help to define what is a story and to give structure to your stories as you begin to learn how to build storytelling into your practice.

The idea of introducing conflict to a story can be challenging, particularly in a business context and is something that participants on my leadership storytelling programmes often struggle with. It is a common theme in many story structures but, of course, if you are wanting to create a story about a change in your organization, you might be nervous about introducing too much conflict! I prefer to think about conflict or adversity like this when working with business storytelling:

- ▷ An acknowledgement that there may be difficult times ahead, and some information on how these difficulties will be dealt with;

- ▷ An element of surprise that the storyteller can introduce to their story, something unexpected from the normal way of communicating change in the organization that will then generate interest; and/or

- ▷ An expression of emotion from the storyteller that will then generate emotion in the listener/reader of the story.

In a business context, it's important to note that any story that you tell as part of a change must have a purpose, that is, it must be linked to something that you are trying to communicate. This is true, too, for stories in other forms of corporate communication. Whilst a story about something that happened to you might be interesting to your colleagues when chatting informally, if it isn't linked to a specific point that you are trying to make in a more formal communication context, it can be seen as simply an anecdote and the power of the story is lost. We will return to this aspect of business storytelling later in the book.

As well as structured stories, more fragmented forms of communication are also used to share information in organizations. David Boje[9] focuses on small chunks of information that become shorthand for shared experiences within teams and organizations. He notes how he saw that just a nod of the head or a single word can sometimes be used in teams to represent an entire story. To those who are in the know at least. Such snippets of stories do not share the elements of the story features outlined earlier and yet Boje argues that the storyteller and listener are co-creating a story based on what they hear and what they already know. They are creating meaning between them and representing something shared about their experiences through the storytelling.

Therefore, the telling of the story is an active event for both the storyteller and the audience of the story, and whilst the story does not need to be necessarily factually true, it has to be believable to the audience.

It's been noted that a story has a sequence that happens in a time and a place, a set of characters and, most importantly, emotions. This can be an element of surprise and/or unanticipated elements and changing emotions throughout the story. Ideally, the story will also move the listener or reader of the story to feel emotions themselves when they experience the story. It is this emotion that is key to making stories memorable and long lasting. Emotions are also important if you are looking to create action through your storytelling.

The celebrated neuroscientist Donald Calne demonstrated that emotions inspire action more than reason in his book *Within Reason*. This is one of the reasons why stories are so important during periods of change. If you are able to describe what people will see and feel during/after change rather than making assertions about what is going to happen, this will inspire more emotion and ultimately more action. There is also a need for truthfulness in this storytelling, enabling the storyteller to share the full range of emotions with the recipient of the story, including pitfalls and challenges that were overcome.

In her work, Jennifer Aaker[10] says that it is important to move your audience intellectually and emotionally with your storytelling, and this is as true for business stories as for any other type of story. Indeed, she discovered that when the same information was conveyed using a story rather than a series of facts, there was a greater level of remembering of the information. In Aaker's study, when listening to presentations, students remembered 63% of a story and only 5% of statistics or facts. Anecdote have also done some interesting work in this area, to explore the link between memory and story, and discovered that stories were seven times more memorable than facts.[11] Imagine being able to harness some of that memory power in your own communication and engagement activities!

So, now that we understand some of the storytelling basics such as story structures (which we will return to again later in this book), let's start moving beyond that to create your own stories that work for you. This is the really exciting part!

In the next section, we turn to the ChangeStories® ARIAS model which will guide you through how you can do this and gather information to create the best possible change story for you and your organization.

PART II
THE
CHANGESTORIES®
ARIAS MODEL

Having read the first few chapters of the book, I hope that you will recognize the pitfalls of some of the traditional change models and are excited to build more storytelling, conversation and inquiry into your practice. Hopefully, you will already have some new ideas to try out.

This next section provides you with the tools to develop your practice further, focusing on five different areas of practice:

- Chapter 3 focuses on paying attention to the things that matter in your organization, both for you as a leader and/or change agent and to employees.

- Chapter 4 considers how important it is to build reflection into daily practice, and how this is particularly important during periods of change.

- Chapter 5 shows how using dialogue, inquiry and conversation during change can lead to a greater understanding of the causes of change resistance and improve change communications.

- Chapter 6 provides an introduction to appreciative inquiry and how we can use this to understand the best from the past and take this forward into the future.

- Chapter 7 shows how to translate everything that you have learnt from the other chapters into a meaningful story about change, which focuses on outcomes and is clear about what the future will look and feel like.

Each chapter includes reflective questions throughout as well as activities to build skills into your daily practice. Links are also included to relevant ChangeStories® podcast episodes.

The model enables us to get underneath the surface in the organization; to recognize change as an individual and dynamic process; to create dialogue and conversation about change, valuing challenge and alternative perspectives and to recognize cultural and historical context, taking an interactive approach to change as it emerges over time.

In fact, the model addresses head on the issues that we discussed earlier in this book which are often forgotten in change programmes. By using the ChangeStories® ARIAS model in your change practice, you will be able to:

▸ Harness change expertise at all levels in your organization;

▸ Identify key change characteristics of individuals, teams and the organization;

▸ Surface hidden stories and artefacts;

▸ Create a more reflective approach to change;

▸ Create successful stories to drive sustainable change.

Using the model is not a one-off exercise but an ongoing, iterative process that should be repeated often during any period of change to have conversations about the things that really matter and ask people for the truth about what it is like to work in the organization at this moment. This inquiry is as important as advocacy during change but leaders and change professionals often focus on advocacy, so, by using the tools in this book, you will automatically be doing something different from the 'normal' approach to change. This will show up as a different approach to change to others in your organization. You will also have the information that you need to create a change story that you can use to explain why the change is happening and to create action.

There are five stages in the ChangeStories® ARIAS model as shown in the illustration. You might be wondering what the choice of images in the model have to do with change and storytelling. Well, the whole model is represented by a group of musicians to illustrate the collaborative nature of change, with people working together to co-create a story and vision for the future. Whilst an aria is usually a solo piece for voice, it is usually accompanied by an orchestra so the images also highlight the performative nature of storytelling and change management with the change specialist/ leader as the conductor orchestrating the journey towards a future state. But the conductor cannot do this on their own, they need their team of musicians to create the future with them.

The images chosen for each of the stages of the model have also been selected with a specific intent. They have been selected to be memorable and unusual. They also tell the story of the model.

The first stage of the model, Attention, has a conductor's baton as its image. A conductor will use their baton to bring the orchestra to attention at the beginning of a piece of music but also to draw their attention to specific moments in an orchestral score. This seemed like the ideal image to represent the first element of the model and the start of the process.

The second stage, Reflection, is represented by a French horn. This is a very shiny, reflective instrument but this is not the reason that this has been chosen! The French horn is well known as being a very difficult instrument to learn and many people also find taking time to reflect difficult. In addition, when a French horn is played as part of an orchestra, reflective screens are placed behind the horn section to reflect the sound forwards and backwards. This is because in an orchestral setting, the horn is meant to be heard as both a direct and indirect sound, and in a room, this will mostly be achieved through reflection.

The third stage, Inquiry, is shown as a piece of musical score. When a musician receives a new musical score and has to learn it, they spend time inquiring and connecting with the piece and the notation until they are able to play it fluently. This stage of the model also involves asking questions and investigating the context of the organization before using this understanding to develop a fluent and compelling change story.

The fourth stage of the model, Appreciation, is represented by a rose. Traditionally, long-stemmed roses (often as a single flower) are given to musicians and performers at the end of the performance to show how the audience appreciates their work.

Finally, the last stage of the model, Storytelling, is represented by a microphone, illustrating the performative nature of storytelling.

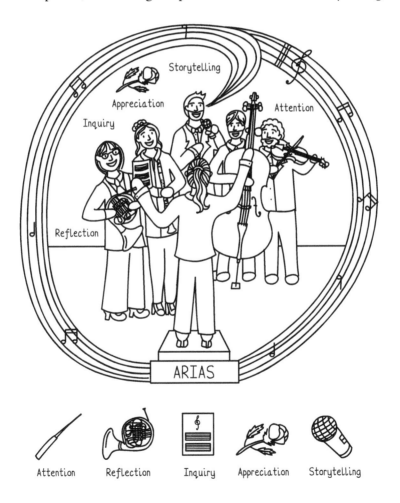

| Attention | Reflection | Inquiry | Appreciation | Storytelling |

Chapter 3
Attention

If you are anything like me, you will sometimes finish a day and wonder what you did and achieved in it. A day can fly past without us paying attention to it. At work, this is especially true, when we have days which are whirlwinds of meetings, Zoom calls and fire fighting. The same is true of working on a change project, where we can sometimes feel like we live by a project plan rather than taking time to take stock and pay attention to what is around us. Organizations are increasingly 'noisy' places where it can be hard to pause and pay attention.

And yet, paying attention to what matters around us is incredibly important for enabling us to understand our organization and to create better change. In this chapter, we will consider the following areas to build greater attention and awareness:

- ▷ Becoming aware of yourself as a leader and change agent and the impact that you have on others;

- ▷ Increasing awareness of what matters to people in your organization;

- ▷ Paying attention and listening to what is going on around you.

Becoming aware of yourself and your impact

As well as paying attention to what is around us, attention is also about having greater levels of self-awareness and the impact we can have on others. This is particularly important for leaders in organizations and forms an essential part of being an authentic leader. I will mention leaders and leadership a lot in this section; however, I believe that these principles apply to anyone in organizations and so these principles are equally as relevant to change professionals and consultants who support organizations through change as well as employees experiencing change.

There is a need for honest and open conversations in organizations in order to build trust and engagement during periods of change. However, honesty, openness, authenticity and vulnerability are often sadly lacking in organizations, particularly at the leadership level. This can come from a place of fear where leaders are reluctant to reveal too much of themselves or are uncomfortable with sharing what they perceive to be 'bad news'. But, by not showing up authentically, leaders are reducing their impact and their ability to introduce change and engage their teams. For example, research conducted by Alavi and Bell[1] and Bakari et al[2] has highlighted that authentic leaders are more able to take people with them when they want to introduce change and win over the hearts and minds of others. The research suggests that this is because authentic leadership behaviours positively influence employee attitudes and beliefs about change and make it more likely that employees will participate in change efforts and create a coalition around the change.

Coetsee emphasizes this point still further: '[T]he authenticity and attitude of [a] leader [is] the crucial factor in winning the hearts and minds of employees in order to create successful change in an organization, rather than the use of an existing change management model.'[3]

What does this mean in the context of change?

Whilst the idea of authentic leadership has been part of the business landscape for some time, it is perhaps misunderstood. The term authentic leadership is often used to suggest a leader who:

▶ Shows that they are trustworthy by being honest and open about admitting and taking responsibility for mistakes;

▶ Has high levels of self-awareness and is happy to share their learning journey with others;

▶ Shows courage to challenge the status quo;

▶ Truly empowers others;

▶ Shares something of their true selves at work.

This approach has been criticized by some as being too simplistic. As Herminia Ibarra writes in the *Harvard Business Review*,[4] having a limited understanding of authentic leadership and trying to apply it in every situation, can backfire. For example, as highlighted in the article, there are risks associated with being totally transparent in all situations. According to Ibarra, there is a trade off between behaving in a way that is expected in a specific situation and behaving in a way that feels authentic. For many leaders, being themselves at work is something that is challenging and a bit scary. However, there is a need for authentic leaders who can share something of their real self in the workplace.

But does this mean being totally honest and open all of the time?

The answer to that is no.

Authentic leadership does not mean simply telling everyone who will listen your innermost secrets. In fact, as Bill George (one of the original thinkers about authentic leadership) says, authentic leadership is mindfully revealing yourself complete with your flaws, but within boundaries.[5] Brené Brown[6] argues that authenticity 'requires almost constant vigilance and awareness about the connections between our thoughts, emotions and behaviours. It also means staying mindful about our intentions. Real authenticity actually requires major self monitoring...'

Being aware of our desire and intentions about authenticity as well as how we might impact on others is important here. Research carried out by Newcastle University Business School in 2013[7] suggests that leaders who are more aware of their own ways of thinking about change and how this might influence others are more likely to be able to lead successful change. Crucially, however, many leaders lack the ability to see how people experience them as a leader.

This process of development as an authentic leader can take a lifetime and is a continual process of learning and growth. There are plenty of ways for us to become more self-aware, including the use of 360 degree feedback and personality questionnaires, as well as engaging a coach or mentor to support us. Sometimes, it can be as simple as paying attention to the way in which people respond to you in meetings and one-to-ones, and reviewing and acting on this feedback. You can use the activity below to help you to analyse any feedback that you receive.

Activity – The feedback lens

When making sense of any feedback that you receive, it can be useful to theme things together through a number of lenses:

▸ What are the areas of consistency between the different sources of feedback that you have gathered (own reflection and feedback from others)?

▸ What are the gaps in this feedback? In particular, identify any feedback from others that feels hard to hear. Think about why that might be and how you could work on those areas.

▸ What are your blind spots? These are strengths that you didn't realize that you had that others can see. What is it that you didn't realize about yourself and how can you build on these strengths?

Increasing your awareness of what matters

Your organization is changing all the time. What is important to people in your organization is also changing all the time. Do you remember when we were told not to leave sat navs in the car? And even not to leave marks on the windscreen from a sat nav holder… in case someone saw it and decided to break in to steal the sat nav. Is that still a thing? I suspect not, as many people will have a sat nav on their phone. And thieves are probably more interested in stealing actual cars these days. Everything changes, and so what worked in the past isn't going to work this time when you want to create change. What to do about it?

Become more aware of what matters in the organization. I've already mentioned the importance of looking forwards and backwards when creating change, to acknowledge the importance of the past as well as planning for the future. Also, the more you pay attention to and listen to stories and information in organizations, the more patterns and themes will emerge that you can then use in your planning for change – as Charles Duhigg says, 'if you listen to enough stories, patterns emerge that were once hidden.'[8] Part of becoming more aware of these stories that emerge in organizations is to listen to what is going on in the organization. But there are also tools that you can use to help start conversations about what matters to people.

A tool that I regularly use is the SOAR model. This is an appreciative version of a SWOT (Strengths, Weaknesses, Opportunities, Threats) analysis, with a focus on strengths rather than weaknesses, and I have found this to be an invaluable way to find out more about organizations and what matters to the people in them. The SOAR model focuses on how things are now and how the team would like them to be in the future and so can be a really positive exercise for teams and individuals.

Activity – SOAR analysis

To complete a SOAR analysis, ask yourself or others the following questions and note down ideas for each element:

▷ Strengths – what are we good at?

▷ Opportunities – what can we do better?

▷ Aspirations – what do we care deeply about?

▷ Results – how will we know that we are succeeding?

The activity is a useful way to create space for attention during a busy working day but also provides an opportunity for engagement with a change programme. As a leader and change professional, the outputs of this exercise will also provide inputs and themes to the creation of any story that you might want to tell about the change.

Paying attention and listening

Taking time to listen and pay attention is another important part of change practice. This includes paying attention to your own thoughts and feelings and also to what is going on around you. Think back to the story that I shared in an earlier chapter about the Christmas decorations. If a leader in this organization had paid attention to the conversations and stories that were being told about the fact that the decorations were still under the stairs, they could have addressed this head on in their change communications and ultimately made the change easier both for the change agents and leaders and, most importantly, to the employees themselves.

I was reminded of this need to pay attention recently when I attended an event that made reference to Nancy Kline's work, *Time to Think*.[9] This approach requires a coach to pay 'beautiful attention' to the person that they are coaching, which I think is such a lovely phrase. It is about listening with absolute intent, interest and respect, treating the person that you are coaching as the most important person in the world to you in that moment. Listening quietly without interruption and maintaining eye contact, even if the person you are talking to moves their eyes away from yours as they are talking (and thinking). It is a difficult skill to master and takes practice. However, paying this kind of attention, both in a one-to-one situation and in groups, can lead to extraordinary outcomes. As Nancy Kline says, '[L]istening of this calibre ignites the human mind. The quality of your attention determines the quality of other people's thinking.'

If you want to see a great example of this attention in action, watch the film *A Beautiful Day in the Neighbourhood* featuring Tom Hanks. A true example of beautiful attention in practice! In the film, Tom Hanks plays Fred Rogers, a beloved children's television presenter from the US. The other main character is Lloyd Vogel, a journalist played by Matthew Rhys who really doesn't seem to like people very much and is tasked with interviewing Fred Rogers. He is a troubled character but, in the course of the film, his barriers drop and he opens up to Fred Rogers. And Rogers makes a difference to his life. By giving him all of his attention (even if Lloyd didn't really want it). He listens and really hears rather than waiting to talk. It's a lovely film and worth a watch if you want to see what paying true attention to yourself and others really looks and feels like.

Any time spent paying attention and listening to others is not wasted, particularly during periods of change. Nancy Duarte[10] has researched this area and has shown that successful change leaders spend time talking to employees and listening to their responses before taking action. Duarte also talks about undertaking listening tours in places of work where leaders spend time out and about in the workplace, listening to what they hear. Years ago, a similar practice was described to me by my Dad as 'management by walking about' and this still rings true today. The temptation to leap into action is ever present but stopping and paying attention will pay dividends in the long run. This doesn't need to take a lot of time. Even one or two additional conversations can create a difference.

Paying attention becomes more difficult if you are working in a hybrid environment as many of us are these days, with people being in the office and working remotely. I worked on a restructuring project during the later part of the pandemic, which was conducted solely over Zoom. It was very difficult both to communicate information to people but also to gauge how they were feeling, when we could not be in the same room together. We had to put in a lot more time and effort in meeting with people one-to-one on a regular basis (and asking line managers to do the same) so that we could check in regularly. We also ensured that we paid attention in Zoom meetings, with one of the team specifically engaging in watching what was going on in the group, noticing who had their camera on or off, what was being said in the chat and also noticing the body language and facial expressions in the group. This took time and effort and had to be a more conscious process in a hybrid environment.

Being more authentic in your practice and increasing your awareness of what matters will enable you to build key content into your change messaging which ultimately will make your messages more sticky and memorable. Linking back to what matters to people and asking them 'what do you need?' also enables you to demonstrate how any change will resolve the issues that they are facing.

As with all the chapters in this section, we end with some reflective questions and activities to enable you to build attention into your daily practice. You don't have to do all of these in a single session but by asking more questions and paying attention to what you hear and see around you, you are taking the first step towards building your storytelling skills and knowledge.

Building attention into your daily practice

To become more self-aware and to begin to pay attention to your impact on others:

> ▷ Think about your own life story. What experiences have influenced you the most? How do these influence your work now and your leadership style?

▸ Seek honest feedback from as wide a circle of people as possible and listen to what they say. This could be using formal processes or simply asking for feedback from people in whatever form works for you.

▸ Practise tailoring your style to different audiences and groups without compromising your core character.

To pay more attention to what matters in the organization, complete a SOAR analysis and also reflect on:

▸ What is the history of the organization and how does it impact on the organization now?

▸ What does this mean for how change can be enacted in the organization?

▸ What is the purpose for the team and does everyone understand this purpose?

▸ How do we want our team to be experienced by others in the organization (and outside)?

To think about change in your organization, try answering these questions yourself and then also discuss them with your team:

▸ What is changing and what does success look like? For the organization? For my team?

▸ How does this change affect my team's needs, activities, behaviours and decisions?

▸ How big does this change feel to my team?

▸ When will they have to start making changes?

▸ What are the obstacles and risks of creating this change? What will my team see as the obstacles?

▷ What emotions and reactions can I expect from my team in relation to this change?

Look for patterns and themes in the responses from your team and consider how to use these to inform your approach to change. Is there anything unexpected that you uncovered which might indicate some hidden factors that you need to consider?

If you are concerned that people are fearful about change, the following questions are useful to open up the discussion in a non-threatening way:

▷ What makes you scared or nervous about this change?

▷ Thinking about your previous experiences of change, what was the most productive thing you did to help you deal with the change?

▷ What tips would you give to others going through change?

▷ What pitfalls would you warn yourself or others of when going through change?

▷ What do you need from me to feel ready for this change?

These questions are useful to uncover what assumptions people are making about change generally, and about a specific change:

▷ Why do think this change is important to our business?

▷ How do you think our team will be impacted by the change?

▷ How do you think you personally will be impacted?

▷ How can we make the most of the change?

▷ How can we work together to make sure change goes smoothly?

▷ How can we keep informed about the change?

ChangeStories® podcast episodes focusing on attention

- ▶ Episode 18 – Susanna Liller. Becoming the heroine (or hero) of our own story.

- ▶ Episode 31 – Susie Palmer-Trew. Creating change that is responsive and respectful to the people in the organization.

Chapter 4
Reflection

In common with paying attention, creating time to reflect is another activity that is often forgotten about in our busy lives. I've been reflecting on reflection recently. Mainly because I have been very busy and have lacked time during the day to truly reflect on my work. This has led me to reflecting in the evenings, sometimes in the middle of the night, which has not been good news for me getting a full night's sleep. This is a common issue for many people at work, despite there being a lot of evidence to show that time to reflect is really important for us to learn, review and reconfigure.

In this chapter, we will consider some of the consequences of not taking time to reflect as well as the skills and behaviours needed to build greater attention and awareness:

- Dysfunctional momentum;

- Change fatigue;

- Creating time to reflect;

- Building change resilience through reflection.

Dysfunctional momentum

I really love an article in the *MIT Sloan Management Review* by Michelle A. Barton and Kathleen M. Sutcliffe[1] which puts lessons learnt from teams fighting wildfires into a business context. I was particularly struck by the focus on pausing and reflecting, instead of simply ploughing on regardless of what is happening around you. The authors use the term 'dysfunctional momentum' to describe this act of continuing along a certain path without asking yourself whether it is the right thing to do. As the authors state, 'dysfunctional momentum... occurs when people continue to work toward an original goal without pausing to recalibrate or reexamine their processes, even in the face of cues that suggest they should change course.' There is a need to take time to reflect to avoid getting stuck in a pattern of thinking. This statement really spoke to me and felt so true of many change programmes that I have experienced.

I wonder if you feel the same?

In many change programmes, the need to continue to follow the critical path or the project plan often overrides the realization that perhaps things are not moving in the right direction. As Barton and Sutcliffe say in their article, 'interruptions – not necessarily of operations but of the thought processes based on assumptions that may no longer be valid – provide an opportunity to question the ongoing story.' It takes courage to do this, though, in the face of usual business practice. But there are many benefits to pausing during a change programme, particularly if the programme is not going well.

I had a powerful example of this on a change programme that I worked on a few years ago. I was asked to review the programme and make suggestions for how it could be improved as it was not progressing as well as the programme manager wished. I spent time with each of the stakeholders on the programme to see how they thought things were going and what suggestions they could make for improvements. Whilst they had lots of suggestions, which were then implemented, one of the most interesting aspects of this exercise was how much the stakeholders valued being asked the question. The programme had ceased activity whilst I conducted my work so this activity also gave the programme team time to take stock of how things were going.

Based on this, as part of the project plan, we built in pauses every six weeks where I discussed the programme with each of the key stakeholders to get their feedback. Based on the themes emerging from this feedback, which were fed back into the change programme, we could make changes to communications, activities and approach to reflect these themes. There was time built into the plan for recalibration and reset. And the pause gave everyone time to reflect and learn lessons. It was a great success and led to a programme that had higher levels of engagement. I try to do this on every programme that I work on now and, even if to begin with it feels like a strange process for people who aren't used to it, people do quickly get on board once they can see the benefits of doing so. This is particularly important on a lengthy programme of change, such as a technology implementation, where the project team can easily become burnt out over the long duration of the project. And employees can become very fatigued by the constant change.

Change fatigue

Change fatigue is often talked about in relation to changes in organizations that are continuous and is a state of exhaustion by employees after having to repeatedly adjust to new ways of working. It is characterized as a lack of enthusiasm towards change or feelings of resistance to further changes. Resistance is a topic that we will come back to later in this book but I am sure that everyone can relate to the feeling of 'oh no, not again' when a new change programme is announced!

Change fatigue can be caused by a number of factors:

- ▶ The speed and frequency of how changes are introduced which can lead to feelings of overwhelm and powerlessness in employees;

- ▶ Poor communication and engagement leading to employees not understanding why more change is being introduced and feeling that they can't control the outcome of the change on them as individuals;

- ▶ A history of previous changes in the organization which didn't deliver what they promised or were handled poorly, leading to distrust amongst employees. This is particularly problematic if the new activity is similar to what went before. For example, a new piece of technology which claims to fix the same problem as the previous one.

Everything that we talk about in this book will help reduce change fatigue and make any future change efforts feel different to what has gone before. Great news! And reflection is a very key part of that, to make sure that you understand what has gone wrong in the past and avoid these mistakes next time.

As an example, on a recent transformation programme that I worked on, leaders were concerned about how fatigued the employees would be after years of new IT systems and ways of working to contend with. I undertook a series of focus group discussions with people across the organization, at all levels, to understand how they felt about the change and gathered some really interesting stories and themes.

What stood out most strongly was the seemingly relentless nature of the changes, with no chance to pause and reflect between each new thing. This is something that I hear time and time again – that people have reached saturation point with change. Interestingly, one of the aspects of the experience that people most valued was the chance to go to the focus group, take time away from their desk and reflect on how they were feeling. This was actually more useful to people than what was actually talked about in the meeting. Taking time to reflect was so valuable to these individuals.

As a result of this work, we used what was dubbed a 'stealthy change' approach on the programme where, instead of announcing one big change, the changes took place as a series of small, continuous improvements with pauses in between. Looking back on it, I'm not sure that stealthy change is quite the right phrase as it feels slightly manipulative, but hopefully doesn't detract from the principle of regular pauses and reflections throughout a change programme to recalibrate and reconnect and avoid moving forward in a dysfunctional way.

We introduced key change messages into everyday communications and conversations rather than in specific messages. I spent a lot of time talking to individual teams and managers to understand the needs of their team and then tailoring the change interventions and communications to suit. I attended lots of team meetings and talked about what was going to happen rather than sending people to attend a specific change programme training course as had been the case in the past. This approach really seemed to work with good engagement from employees and managers.

The feelings of powerlessness and lack of control that employees experience during a change can have a major impact on performance and productivity during any change programme. Reflecting on this and talking about change in a different way can really pay dividends.

David Rock (in his brilliant book, *Your Mind at Work*) has developed the SCARF model for thinking about collaborative working, using insights from neuroscience and how we react to threats and rewards. In the context of change, we can use this model to help us to shape how we talk about and communicate change. The SCARF model includes five factors which represent how we experience the world around us (in relation to ourselves):

- ▶ Status – how important we feel in relation to others;

- ▶ Certainty – how we feel we can predict the future;

- ▶ Autonomy – how much control we feel we have over events;

- ▶ Relatedness – how safe we feel with others and how we feel that we belong;

- ▶ Fairness – how fair we feel our exchanges with others are.

If, during a period of change, we feel that any of these factors are going to be impacted by the change, this can lead to disengagement and fear – all typical of an organization where change fatigue is an issue. Therefore, when creating any communication about a change, it is useful to consider whether an employee will be able to answer the following statements as a result of the communication/ change activity:

- ▶ Status – 'I feel valued'

- ▶ Certainty – 'I know what is going to happen'

- ▶ Autonomy – 'I feel in control'

▹ Relatedness – 'I know how I fit in and what I have to do next'

▹ Fairness – 'I feel that I am being treated with respect'

Reflecting on any communications that are planned and using these questions as a checklist to review your actions will ensure that you are creating materials and activities that respond to individual needs and will result in the highest possible chance of engagement rather than disengagement.

Pausing and reflecting during change is a key part of the ChangeStories® ARIAS model, and although it is here as a key stage in the process as a reminder to take time to reflect right at the beginning of a change, it is essential to ensure there is time to reflect at every stage of change to get under the surface of the organization and understand the factors that accelerate or anchor change in every part of the organization.

But how can we build time to think, reflect and listen into our own daily life, at work and at home?

Creating time to reflect

Shortening meetings from 60 minutes to 45 minutes (or even 30 minutes) gives time to think and reflect between Zoom calls and/ or meetings and more time to focus. Also, blocking time out in your diary, and being really strict about keeping it free, gives you time to think and plan rather than constantly 'doing'. The concept of 'deep work' is important here, creating time that is distraction-free to focus on creating new ideas and develop skills.

The chess fans reading this will know that Deep Thought was a computer developed to play chess against the best (human) chess players in the world. Science fiction aficionados will know that Deep Thought was named after the computer with the same name from *The Hitchhiker's Guide to the Galaxy* which came up with the answer to life, the universe and everything. Two computers which were excellent at thinking deeply. If only we found it easy to do the same. I, like many others, sometimes struggle to find the time to think deeply about things.

These 'things' could be spending time reflecting on my work, coming up with new and creative ideas and even focusing on my own development. And that is a problem.

It has been claimed that our attention spans have been reduced through a diet of social media, on-demand television and political discourse reduced to the length of a tweet. However, it's not that our attention spans have been reduced, it's just that there is so much information around and we have had to become better at filtering out the dross and focusing on what we find important and/or interesting. After all, we have no problem binge watching Netflix, but we might struggle to sit at our desks long enough to develop a change readiness plan.

It seems that in order to focus on something, we have to make it interesting enough for us to devote ourselves to it. And we also need to give ourselves the time and space to do it, which of course can also be difficult. There is some great advice on doing more deep work in Cal Newport's excellent book, *Deep Work*.[2]

For some people, taking time to reflect can feel uncomfortable and difficult, particularly if it is not something that they do often. My advice would be to start small, giving yourself five minutes to reflect after each meeting or after each task you complete. Find the time of day that works for you and schedule time for reflection then. Get rid of or shut down as many distractions as you can, including notifications for emails, social media etc. Or take time to reflect whilst doing something else. I love to swim and find that my mind can easily wander and reflect whilst I'm swimming up and down. I often have some of my best ideas whilst I am in the pool! And walking can be an excellent way to reflect by yourself or with others.

As Peter Drucker said: 'Follow effective action with quiet reflection. From the quiet reflection, will come even more reflective action.'

There are some reflective questions at the end of this chapter to give you some more ideas on building reflection into your daily practice.

Building change resilience

As we have seen, enabling employees to understand and feel comfortable about a change reduces change fatigue and increases engagement. Beyond this, there is a need to build resilience to change and taking an approach of continual evolution and reflection rather than major change programmes followed by periods of stability is the best way of doing this.

Change resilience is the opposite of change fatigue and enables individuals and teams to cope with and adapt to change. Thinking back to Bridge's model of transition, it creates an environment where people can move on from the past, embrace new ways of working and look to the future with energy.

To create an environment where change resilience can thrive, an individual, team or organization needs to:

▷ Accept that change is a part of everyday life in an organization and is an opportunity to grow and learn;

▷ Create a safe environment in teams and organizations to enable people to share their fears and ideas (psychological safety in other words – we will come onto this in the next chapter);

- ▶ Provide opportunities to listen, talk and have open, honest and courageous conversations about change;

- ▶ Encourage self-awareness at all levels, particularly of your own and other people's individual reactions to change;

- ▶ Promote daily kindness to yourself and others during a period of change, acknowledging that it can be a difficult time for people;

- ▶ Provide support systems including colleagues, mentors and professional support to provide guidance during difficult times;

- ▶ Celebrate success and identify and reward people who role model change resilience;

- ▶ Commit to practices that help people manage stress and maintain wellbeing;

- ▶ Respect that everyone deals with change differently.

There are lots of ideas in this book for creating a safe environment with conversation and inquiry at its heart. You can also consider your own resilience (and encourage others to do the same) by creating your own resilience plan.

Activity – Creating a resilience plan

Understanding more about our own resilience is an important part of dealing with the impact of change. Think about:

- ▶ What saps my resilience? For example, too many things to do, uncertainty, technology distractions etc.

▶ What restocks my resilience? For example, talking about my worries, making sure that I sleep and eat well etc.

▶ What are the signs that I am becoming less resilient? For example, changes to appetite, changing moods, lack of sleep etc.

▶ What can I do to maintain my resilience? What are the three key actions that I can do today to make a difference?

You can also run this as a discussion in a team or small group. If you decide to do this, ask the group to work together to develop ideas for resilience. It can also be useful to share signs that resilience is being damaged as this enables teams to look out for each other and prompt individuals to return to their resilience plan to restock their resilience.

In her podcast conversation with me, Rebecca Mander shared her approach to building resilience and one of the key areas we talked about was challenging the stories that we tell ourselves about ourselves. You might be familiar with imposter syndrome (also known as the imposter phenomenon) which can make us doubt our abilities to deal with new things, and at the root of this is the voice on our shoulder telling us stories about how we can't do things. Rebecca shared her approach to stopping these stories by focusing on the evidence in front of us, and when we hear our internal voice telling us one of these stories, asking ourselves 'is this true?'. I use this technique all the time when my inner voice starts dragging me down. If you want to find out more about Rebecca's approach, there is a detailed explanation on how to do that in the podcast episode, which is linked at the end of this chapter.

Building reflection into your daily practice

Before you start reflecting, it is useful to think about how you can make it a regular practice.

- When do you have the most energy and time to reflect? First thing in the morning, at lunch time, before bed or throughout the day? Then schedule this into your diary in five- to ten-minute chunks to begin with.

- What tools do you need to help you to reflect? Notebook and pen? Notes on your phone, voice notes, in an app? The ways to do this are endless so experiment and find the tool that works best for you. I find a notebook with plain rather than lined paper works for me and discovered this after many years of trying to like journaling. It wasn't until I used plain paper that I actually did it regularly and enjoyed it.

- Where is the best place for me to reflect? At work or at home? Indoors or outdoors? As I said earlier, I get a lot of my best ideas whilst doing something else such as swimming or walking the dog. I think physical activity that I don't have to think too much about frees my mind up and creates space for reflection and innovation.

- Are there podcasts, radio or television programmes that stimulate your thinking? When you listen or watch to these, can you take a few minutes to reflect afterwards about what you are taking away from these experiences?

- Where can I link this into existing activities and routines? James Clear in his brilliant book *Atomic Habits* talks about habit stacking as a way to create a good habit in the easiest manner possible. Is there a way that you can link reflection to something that you already do? Could you do it whilst you have a coffee, on your commute or in the lift? By linking it back to a habit that is already part of your routine it will become easier to maintain.

Here are some example prompt questions to get started on your reflection:

▸ What did I learn or discover today?

▸ What challenged me, and how did I cope with it?

▸ What am I curious about exploring further?

▸ How did my actions impact others?

▸ What can I do tomorrow to improve?

Don't be limited by these questions. Create questions that will work for you and give you the time and space that you need.

Also, start really small with this if this is not a practice that you are used to. Five minutes per day is better than nothing. It's easy to feel overwhelmed by having yet another thing to do but just a few minutes to think between meetings will make such a difference to how you and others around you deal with change. The key is to be consistent and create as much space to reflect as you can. And also make sure that you are giving other people their own space to reflect.

ChangeStories® podcast episodes focusing on reflection

▸ Episode 10 – Lorraine Checklin. Mindfulness and reflective techniques for the workplace.

- Episode 11 – Rebecca Mander. Bouncing forward from setbacks, seeking support and self-knowledge, understanding your strengths and building resilience.

- Episode 13 – Sue Cox. Understanding the neuroscience of addiction and how to take better care of our brains.

- Episode 35 – Susan Ní Chríodaín. Being ready to speak and tell your story.

- Episode 43 – Alison Jones. The transformative power of exploratory writing.

Chapter 5
Inquiry

The psychologist Manfred Kets de Vries recounts a Sufi tale in his book *Organizations on the Couch*.[1] In this story, a man notices a lump under a rug which he tries in vain to flatten before lifting the rug to find a snake. Kets de Vries uses this story as a metaphor for trying to create change in organizations, where organizations try to implement interventions to deal with issues without understanding the underlying problem.

This metaphor is worth remembering for all of us who work to enact change within organizations. Many years ago, I did an organization design project within a local government organization. We were tasked with creating a new structure for the whole organization and so had to review all the existing structure charts. Discussing these charts with key stakeholders, it was interesting to note how many roles had been created to deal with difficult working relationships.

In many organizations, the structures and processes that can be seen are only a tiny fraction of the unseen and hidden factors underneath, as has already been discussed. Digging down into these hidden layers is an integral part of the ChangeStories® ARIAS model. I think this process is like undertaking an archaeological dig – scraping away the layers of the soil that you can see to get to the treasure beneath.

In this chapter, we will consider the different aspects of inquiry that enable us to dig below the surface and look under the rug, focusing on these areas:

- Ongoing inquiry and engagement;

- Having uncomfortable conversations;

- Asking the important questions;

- Rethinking change resistance.

Ongoing inquiry and engagement

Change practitioners and leaders often conduct a stakeholder analysis at the start of the change process to determine how to engage with each group throughout the change. But how many organizations repeat this exercise throughout a change programme? Going back to the group that I met with regularly as part of my PhD research, their views shifted over the period of the project. By meeting with them regularly and listening to their stories, I was able to see this movement and I realized the importance of asking questions and inquiring on an ongoing basis. It is likely that this pattern of identity shift happens in other organizations and so it is important to engage deeply with stakeholders frequently during periods of change.

This process of inquiry is often missing in organizations facing change. Think back to the last change that you were involved with or experienced. I bet that a lot of the communications and engagement activity focused on selling the benefits of the change to stakeholders, rather than asking questions about what they needed. We spend a lot of time advocating for the change rather than inquiring about whether the change is needed and how it will impact on people. In episode 16 of the ChangeStories® podcast, my guest, Alan Arnett, uses a great analogy of change as being like a shiny pen. Typically, we spend our time trying to sell the shiny pen to people rather than asking them whether they actually need a pen. And, if they do need a pen, we don't understand what sort of pen is going to help them the most. I think about the shiny pen image often when I am working in organizations!

This ongoing process should also involve listening to and gathering stories from the organization, as we have previously discussed. Gathering stories from people in organizations can feel time-consuming and creates a lot of data. But it also gives a deep insight into how people are thinking and feeling during a period of change. Change is messy and difficult to manage and so using stories to get underneath the organizational rhetoric is useful in understanding some of this messiness. Yiannis Gabriel talks about this as the 'unmanaged organization,'[2] the part of the organization that is not under its control. The snakes under the rug, so to speak.

Having uncomfortable conversations

It's obvious really that asking questions and listening to stories is important during change, and yet it is often not an activity during a change programme. In my experience, part of this is a fear of being asked difficult questions and/or a fear of having to have difficult conversations. So, leaders and change professionals can sometimes choose not to even have these conversations and focus on advocacy for change rather than inquiry about what people need and how the change can help them. Leandro Herrero[3] likens organizations with a strong focus on advocacy as 'permanent focus groups', where everyone is telling each other what to do rather than becoming activists by having conversations and solving problems together.

There's a lot of content out there about how to have difficult conversations. These often focus on tools and techniques to plan and prepare and how to be during the conversation. Whilst these guides can be useful, framing these conversations as being difficult is one of the reasons that these conversations simply don't happen.

By seeing these conversations as difficult, people avoid them.

It can't be denied that some conversations can be uncomfortable but... is discomfort such a bad thing?

After all, often the experiences that lead to our greatest learning and growth are the most uncomfortable.[4] Reframing such conversations as an opportunity for learning on both sides can lead to a more honest conversation as both parties will approach the conversation with an open mind. Which might lead to an actual conversation rather than simply talk.

This might seem like a strange distinction but talk takes up a lot of our time and talk adds very little value to either us as individuals or to the organization as a whole.[5] In contrast, a real conversation is founded in awareness: of self, of the other, of being present in the moment and of how both parties can be changed in and by the conversation.[6]

Part of undertaking true inquiry, then, is to be aware of how uncomfortable we feel about doing it and to consider why this is. Going back to feeling uncomfortable and learning again, part of having more real inquiry is to sit with that uncomfortable feeling and ask yourself why you are feeling uncomfortable.

Maybe this uncomfortableness is a fear of emotions?

Fear about how the other party might react?

A fear of getting it wrong?

A fear of upsetting people?

Whatever the reason for the fear, instead of avoiding inquiry, creating true change requires us to go ahead and do it as best we can, acknowledging mistakes that we might make as we go along. My great friends and fellow storytellers David Lee and Susan Ní Chríodaín both write and speak about the need for having courageous conversations, expressing ourselves and allowing others to do the same. David also notes how the stories that we tell ourselves about how these conversations might go get in our way of actually managing to do it. Take a listen to their podcast episodes which are listed in this section.

Instead of framing conversations as difficult, we have a responsibility to frame all conversations as important and to develop confidence in having real conversations. This means developing these skills and behaviours:

- Listening and asking questions;
- Showing up with your whole self, facing your thoughts, emotions and behaviours head on;
- Creating capacity and confidence in ourselves and others to have these conversations;
- Being present in the moment of the conversation;
- Noticing what is going on in the conversation;

▷ Allowing space for the conversation to flow – be slow, mindful and reflective;

▷ Not being afraid of emotions.

Much of my work is rooted in appreciative inquiry, and the late, great Jane Magruder Watkins used the mantra 'plan tight, hang loose' to describe how to prepare for an appreciative inquiry session.[7] There will be a lot more information and discussion about appreciative inquiry in the next chapter but this is a useful reminder here too.

Do some planning if that makes you feel more comfortable about the conversation, but don't stick to it no matter what. Be guided by the other person in the conversation with you. Above all, remember that this is not all about you. There are two of you in this conversation. Keep your focus on the other person more than yourself. How can the conversation help both of you to develop and grow?

And if it doesn't go right first time, pause, reflect, get help and try again.

Asking the important questions

Leaning into being uncomfortable is a key part of inquiry as it will encourage you to have more of the conversations that previously felt difficult. But that is only part of the process. It is also important to undertake inquiry into the problems for people in the organization and how might the proposed change solve these problems.

Think about the classic supermarket customer service noticeboard, which has a set of questions from customers ('You Asked') followed by statements from the store about what they are going to do about it ('We Did'). How often is this sort of approach used during (or even before) a change programme? And what difference would it make if these sorts of questions were asked right at the beginning?

There are a few key questions that need to be asked (and answered) right at the beginning of a change programme:

- What are the key issues for you in this organization right now?

- How does this change programme help to solve these issues?

- Why are we doing this change?

- And why are we doing this now?

As a side note, if the change programme is not helping to solve these issues *at all*, it's probably worth asking a supplementary question about whether the change is actually needed. For example, on a recent technology change that I worked on, for most of the organization it was a positive change. A move away from clunky technology and spreadsheet-based processes to a better, more modern system. However, in one part of the organization, a different technology was already used and the new system represented a step backwards. We had to be very careful about how we talked about the benefits of change as these benefits were not consistent across the organization. It's back to the shiny pen analogy again. Figure out what people need and then talk to them about how the change will help them. And if it isn't going to solve all their problems, be honest that this is the case.

Critical to making this work is creating an environment where people feel safe to be open and to speak up when needed, with ideas, questions and concerns. A workplace where colleagues trust and respect each other and people feel able to be candid. This is at the core of psychological safety at work.

Amy Edmondson writes, 'psychological safety is a belief that one will not be punished or humiliated for speaking up with ideas, questions, concerns of mistakes'.[8] This is more than just a fluffy, nice-to-have in an organization. This makes a real impact to the bottom line.

A Gallup poll in 2017[9] found that only 30% of employers agreed that they met this bar. If 60% met the bar, Gallup calculated that there would be a 27% reduction in employee turnover, a 40% reduction in safety incidents and a 12% increase in productivity. Using inquiry-based tools during change increases the opportunity for people to speak up and be heard, invites genuine participation and reduces the impact of resistance.

To understand more about how to do this in practice, I really like Edgar Schein's book, *Humble Inquiry*. He defines 'humble inquiry' as 'the fine art of drawing someone out, of asking questions to which you do not already know the answer, and of building a relationship based on curiosity and interest in the other person'. The words that are most important in that sentence are curiosity and interest. It is impossible to ask the right questions unless you are genuinely interested in the answer and give the other person time to answer.

As with the previous section about uncomfortable conversations, there is a need for openness here too. An openness to emotion, different perspectives and views. And also a need to suspend judgement whilst carefully listening to the response to your question.

Difficult skills perhaps, but ones that can be learnt with practice. We've already talked about noticing and paying attention and you can really use that here as you develop your inquiry skills. Notice when you interrupt (or want to interrupt) someone who is speaking to you. Listen to your own thoughts as you start wondering what to say next when you should be listening to someone else. Bring yourself back into the moment, paying attention to what is happening right now. Be comfortable with silence rather than jumping straight in with a response. Allow yourself to be comfortable with being uncomfortable.

Dr John Launer, one of the founders of narrative medicine in the UK (who spoke about inquiry wonderfully on the ChangeStories® podcast), notes the need for 'weaving a tapestry, not digging a hole' when conducting a true inquiry. This is a key difference – you want to use questions to move the conversation forward rather than simply getting into the detail. I loved this distinction and imagery when I heard it for the first time and still do today. He emphasized many times during our conversation the importance of listening carefully during inquiry, almost like a literary scholar would with a text. Paying attention to cues, words that are usually ignored and also words that are not being said. Asking questions to invite change and 'destabilizing yourself enough to be curious.'

It can take time to perfect this, and in fact, if this does not come naturally to you, it can take a lifetime. I know about this from personal experience, as this is something that I really find difficult. But, trust me, it is really worth the effort!

Rethinking change resistance

A lot of leaders fear engaging or asking questions in case they find out things that they don't want to hear. But, if we reframe resistance, it can be a useful additional source of information.

Recently I've been thinking about or perhaps rethinking change resistance. When I first started out working in organization change, resistance was seen as a difficult behaviour perpetuated by difficult people. Every day I saw managers and change agents battling to overcome resistance to change, often without success. I heard plenty of stories about people being resistant and doing resistant acts (for example, the toilet roll story at the beginning of the book). I also met people who took pride in their resistance to change, including one individual who described himself to me as an 'organizational terrorist' who just wanted to cause disruption and delay to any change programme. Until relatively recently, I had a negative view towards people who would not engage with a change.

Then one day, when I started conducting my own research into organization change, I discovered that individual resistance to change was dynamic. Someone who resisted the change at one point in a change programme could become a supporter of the programme at a later date. This had nothing to do with any activity to reduce their level of resistance. Instead, it came from how they felt about the organization at that time and how they saw their role in it. On any particular day. Because of this I realized that instead of being a negative thing, perhaps change resistance represents the ultimate level of engagement in change.

After all, why would someone work so hard to resist something if they weren't emotionally invested in it? In some ways, I'd rather have change resistance than change apathy!

Unfortunately, resistance has often been typified as the actions of a few 'difficult' individuals – '... a counterproductive irritant for mainstream management thought...' (see Mumby et al's brilliant article called 'Resistance Redux'[10]). Existing research in the field[11] has highlighted different forms of resistance: active, such as striking, or more passive, such as questioning decisions or withholding consent. Resistance may also be organized as a group activity or unorganized and practised by an individual. There are many acts which could be defined as resistance, ranging from those that could disrupt business as usual, such as striking, to individual acts of scepticism about the future direction of an organization.

Researchers have discovered small or micro acts of resistance which, despite being covert, can still lead to delays in introducing organization change. This is '... the classic situation of the go-slow. This is not explicit resistance (as in conventional revolts or strikes) or a mental pulling-out from the professional sphere (as in withdrawal), but a form of deviance which complies with the letter of the law but discreetly resists its spirit. One goes through the motions... the everyday games of the players who discreetly resist, without proclaiming it loud and clear'[12] The more recent phenomenon of quiet quitting is an example of this type of behaviour.

Notice some of the language that has been used in these pieces of research into resistance – deviance, difficult, irritant, revolt. It's no wonder that resistance is perceived so negatively.

The assumption underpinning all of this research is that managers in organizations are able to dictate the actions of others in the organization with little or no opposition to their ideas. And where this opposition does occur, it is caused by resistance. Change resistance is seen as a response to a change which does not fit with what a change agent or leader is trying to achieve. But can we be sure that a behaviour that we see at work is resistance?

The answer to that is a definite 'no.'

What counts as resistance in one situation or organization won't in another.

Often, resistors are seen as tragic characters in opposition to the hero of the piece – the manager or change agent trying to create change. There is an assumption here that individual resistance to change is due to the personal characteristics of the employee. This might be true in some circumstances, depending on the change that is being introduced and how it fits with an individual's personal characteristics. For example, if an individual finds uncertainty difficult to handle, then they may find change harder than an individual who doesn't. But this assumes that everyone feels and acts the same every day, which we know from our own experience isn't true.

Reframing resistance as a necessary and constructive[13] response to change rather than the irrational behaviour of a difficult employee is crucial. As already mentioned, surely if an individual is invested enough in a change to express dissatisfaction or concerns about it, these views are to be welcomed. For any seemingly resistant act or behaviour, it is important to ask, why might this person behave in this way? Engage with them to understand their behaviour and why it occurs. Work with them to understand where they are coming from rather than seeing resistance as something to overcome.

I think it is time to reconsider what change resistance actually is. Instead of being the work of a few disruptive individuals in an organization, we could see it as the work of people who are engaged enough in the change to ask questions rather than just accepting what they are told. People who need more detail about what is going to happen and who aren't satisfied with big-picture thinking. People who want to share their ideas and engage. People who see, hear or tell the story of change in a different way. That is something to be celebrated and encouraged as we try to create a shared story that everyone can get behind.

There is a wonderful 2009 TED Talk by Chimamanda Ngozi Adichie which I return to often, where she discusses the danger of only hearing a single story.[14] In the talk, she reflects that, if you only hear a single story about a place or a person, this leads to stereotypical thinking. She says, '[T]he consequence of the single story is this: it robs people of dignity. It makes our recognition of our equal humanity difficult. It emphasizes how we are different rather than how we are similar.' In organizations, the same is true. If we do not allow different thinking (or resistance) to be heard, we are in danger of only hearing the single story about change in the organization – that is, the story from the change programme and/or from leadership. And this can be dangerous.

We should see resistance as a simple, everyday fact of organizations. Organizations are made up of many different, paradoxical humans who behave differently every day. Rather than trying to control or minimize resistance, we should welcome it as an expression of the diversity of organizations and an integral part of them. This can be scary for leaders and change practitioners who may resist the idea of opening up the floor to others who might disrupt their carefully planned change programme.

It can also be interesting to flip the idea of resistance on its head and look for people in the organization who are influential and could act as champions. These champions are not in the usual model of change agents. Rather they are 'positive deviants' (in the language of the *Harvard Business Review* article where this term comes from[15]) who are influential and who are already working in the ways that are required in the future. There are always pockets of good practice within organizations and finding them and recognizing them is key. As a result of their influence, they are able to act as role models and are also able to speak to their teams to explain what is changing and why.

In her podcast conversation with me, Jude Jennison agreed that it is time to recalibrate what we think about resistance and understand that at the root of it may be fear but also curiosity and reflection. Dialogue is key here to understand what is at the root of a particular action on the part of an employee. Jude also said that there was a wisdom in resistance which should be paid attention to but, sadly, people do not have the time and space in organizations to engage with it. Another indication of the importance of taking time to reflect and pay attention, as well as inquiring into behaviours.

As we all know, change is anything but simple. Change is complex and messy. But, imagine what might happen if we opened our minds to the resistors' point of view...

Imagine if we got the resistors involved in a change programme from the beginning rather than seeing them as an annoying side show that is preventing us from achieving what we want. Imagine if we asked them questions and listened to what they had to say. And used what we learnt to make our change programmes better, more inclusive and more robust.

Imagine if we considered them to be super engagers rather than resistors.

How might that influence the way that we deal with resistance?

And how might that make our organizations more human?

As Cath Bishop states in her wonderful book, *The Long Win*, 'change is not a battle to be won or lost but a collaborative effort to find the best solutions and ideas and unshackle ourselves from the past.'[16]

Building inquiry into your daily practice

If you want to start an inquiry to get beneath the surface of your organization, these questions are useful starting points:

- ▶ Thinking back over your time in the organization, what has happened that has been most interesting?

- ▶ What stories have you heard about the organization relating to past changes?

- What stories did you hear about the organization before you joined it?

- Describe an incident that you witnessed which captures the nature of your experience of working here?

Is there anything unexpected emerging from these questions that might be related to hidden factors in your organization that you need to consider?

The next time you are going into a conversation that makes you feel uncomfortable, think about:

- Do you think that you are in the right and the other person is wrong? Could you frame this differently as 'I have my own point of view but also might be missing something'?

- Do you think the other person is to blame? Could you frame this differently as 'both us of may have contributed in ways that we can't fully see at the moment'?

- Do you want to avoid saying things that might upset or anger the other person? Could you reframe this as seeing a negative reaction as uncomfortable but maybe necessary for progress to be made?

- Do you want to get the other person to see things your way or do you feel that you need to defer to the other person? Could you reframe this as a conversation to create common understandings and a path forward?

If you wish to develop your thinking further, look at David Lee's guidance on having courageous conversations for some fantastic ideas.[17]

But...

Whilst it's good to prepare for a potentially uncomfortable situation, you must also be ready to be responsive to the situation as it unfolds:

- ▶ Notice what is going on in the meeting.
- ▶ How is the other person reacting?
- ▶ How are you reacting?
- ▶ What is interesting about that?

If you are encountering change resistance (within yourself or others), ask yourself what it is that is being resisted:

- ▶ The change itself?
- ▶ The way that it is being implemented?
- ▶ Something else?
- ▶ What can I do to understand their point of view?
- ▶ What changes can I make as a result of what I have learnt from this?

ChangeStories® podcast episodes focusing on inquiry

- ▶ Episode 3 – Ann Knights. Creating change one conversation at a time.
- ▶ Episode 6 – Jon Harding. Creating shared team identity through change.
- ▶ Episode 16 – Alan Arnett. Confessions of a change practitioner.
- ▶ Episode 23 – Cath Bishop. Creating a new story about winning and success.

- Episode 38 – Dr John Launer. Creating conversations that invite change.

- Episode 41 – Jennifer Bryan. It's about people, not rocket science.

Chapter 6
Appreciation

So many of the change programmes that I have worked on seemed to pay little attention to what had happened in the past, apart from conducting a brief 'as is' review of existing processes at the start of the project before moving onto what the future state was going to be. There was very little appreciation of the good bits of the organization that existed and probably didn't really need to change. It's like the old saying of throwing the baby away with the bathwater. If we don't understand and appreciate all the great stuff that is going on in organizations, there is a risk that we throw it away and then have to recreate it. In addition, as already discussed, showing people how things that they value from the past can be taken forward to the future can impact on the acceptance of change.

A key element of the ChangeStories® ARIAS model is appreciating the best of what is, before creating any change. And the activities that have already taken place – attention, reflection and inquiry – give us the information that we need to be able to do that. To help us understand how to be more appreciative, this chapter focuses on:

- The principles of appreciative inquiry;
- Having an appreciative mindset.

Principles of appreciative inquiry

Appreciative inquiry underpins both my academic research and my change management practice. It was first developed by David Cooperrider and Suresh Srivastra[1] as a means to create change in organizations. It is focused on exploring and valuing 'the best of what is' within individuals and organizations in order to unleash potential and success. The key assumption of appreciative inquiry is that within every organization something works well and contributes to success. By using appreciative inquiry, and by gathering stories and having conversations, we can enable organizations and individuals to focus on what works well and then use this to build success for the future.

An element of appreciative inquiry that I really love is the idea that people can work together to dream for the future, identify solutions and positive outcomes, rather than simply highlighting problems. A typical appreciative inquiry involves four stages:

- Discovery – understand the best of what is;
- Dream – envision what could be;
- Design – discuss what should be;

▷ Destiny – initiate what will be. (Adapted from *The Appreciative Inquiry Handbook* by David Cooperrider and Diana Whitney)

Appreciative inquiry is not about only considering the positive in every situation and ignoring the negative. According to Cooperrider and Fry, we should think beyond this polarity and focus instead on 'what gives life, what fuels development potential, what has deep meaning' in organizations. In fact, Cooperrider and Fry's research during the 2020 pandemic[2] shows that disruption can lead to great strides forwards in organizations. We saw this during the pandemic when organizations had to swiftly pivot their service or product offering and/or enable their workforce to quickly work remotely. Individuals and organizations had to be resilient and creative in the way that they approach their work.

Cooperrider and Fry argue that having a strengths-based focus can lead to even greater change than focusing on deficits. They quote a study by Linda Robson[3] that found that the greatest change success emerged when organizations focused 80% of the time on what was working and 20% of the time on what was not working. This led to a four times greater chance of change success. This is a very different approach to many change programmes which focus on everything that is wrong with the organization and how the change programme will fix that rather than focusing on all the good that exists. I certainly saw this happen in my early consultancy career, where we would come in and pick apart everything that existed in the organization and would show how we were going to make everything better. And then we wondered why the employees in the organizations were less than enthusiastic about our suggestions... when basically we had said that everything that had gone before was terrible!

Appreciation can help achieve change during difficult times as it enables us to focus on our strengths and collaborate with others to generate new ideas. Often, when we face change and uncertainty, it is difficult for us to see a way through to the other side. We may feel trapped and helpless and can easily fall into a trap of negative thought. Having an appreciative mindset to support our thinking around the whole situation can avoid these traps and help us to develop new thoughts and engage with new solutions.

Having an appreciative mindset

Having a more appreciative mindset is about shifting the focus from problems to opportunities. It is not about pretending that everything is perfect or that a change process is going to be without challenge. Instead, it is about viewing these challenges through an appreciative lens.

Part of this is paying attention to and noticing the good that is already going on in your organization and in your team, and then thinking of ways to take this forward to the future. Reflecting on and celebrating success is also essential to being more appreciative.

When working with teams and individuals during change, being appreciative is about shifting the perspective of yourself and others and seeing challenge as a way to grow. It can be as simple as reframing some of the ways that you talk about change or ask questions.

We have already discussed the SOAR model, and this is a great way to shift from deficit to possibilities. But, creating an emotional connection at work is also important to create an appreciative environment. There is so little time for this in organizations and yet this can have a huge impact on wellbeing. Helena Clayton, in her podcast conversation with me, talked about the need to slow down to create space for connection, inclusion, trust, collaboration and innovation. A key part of this is appreciation for self and others, enabling everyone to be their best selves at work.

Activity – Start, Stop and Continue

Another useful model is Start, Stop and Continue, which is a well-known appreciative way to review current practices. You can do this as a thought exercise on your own or in groups by considering the following questions:

▸ START – What should I/we start doing? (Think about things that are not being done that should be done or things that are worth trying out for better results);

▸ STOP – What should I/we stop doing? (Think about things that are not working or not helping to deliver desired results as well as things that we or others dislike);

▸ CONTINUE – What should I/we keep doing? (Think about things that are working well, things that we want to keep or things that we like or need).

When I completed one of these exercises with a client recently, they wanted to start focusing on more valued added work, which meant stopping some of the transactional processing of forms that the team were doing. This would give them more time to be more proactive with their internal customers and resolve issues more quickly. Because we were able to focus on what the team wanted to start doing, the team started the exercise in a much more positive frame of mind. This is in comparison to other forms of brainstorming sessions that I have been part of which look at what isn't working so well and then trying to find solutions to these problems. Unfortunately, having a start point of a deficit can mean that the session deteriorates into a huge moaning exercise where everyone leaves the room feeling worse than when they started. Not a great way to build engagement and enthusiasm for something new!

By taking a more appreciative mindset, you will be amazed to see the difference in conversations and engagement that can emerge as a result. Be curious with yourself and others about what lies at the heart of success and how this can be continued into the future.

Building appreciation into your daily practice

To begin thinking about possibilities rather than deficits, ask yourself:

▷ When are we at our best?

▷ What are our top strengths and what are their root causes?

▷ What are our most challenging experiences? (When is/ are our thinking/ideas challenged, values confronted/ emotions provoked/choices questioned?)

▷ What do we want more of?

▷ How else can we handle this?

▷ What needs to happen now?

▷ What one small action would make a difference?

To conduct an appreciative-based inquiry in your organization, mix and match these questions (using a few from each section):

Discovery:

▷ What is working really well?

▷ What is it like to work here right now? (words/pictures)

▷ What has been your best experience of working here?

- What made you feel really part of the organization when you joined?

- What did you like about the organization when you joined?

- What stories have you heard about the organization relating to past, present or future change?

- Describe an incident that you witnessed which captures the nature of your experience of working here.

- What stories did you hear about the organization when you first joined that helped you to understand what it is like?

- What does a good/bad day working here look like?

Dream:

- What are your dreams for the future of the organization? (words/pictures)

- What could this organization learn from other organizations?

- What are the characteristics of people that you particularly admire in the organization?

- Thinking back over your time in the organization, what has happened that has been most interesting from your perspective?

Design:

Based on the outcomes of the 'Dream' discussions:

- What are your top three improvement priorities for the future of the organization?

- What is one thing that we could do to make things better?

▶ What do we care deeply about as an organization?

Destiny:

▶ What innovative actions could be completed to help this organization improve?

▶ How will we know that we are succeeding?

▶ How have you/the organization changed since the beginning of the process?

ChangeStories® podcast episodes focusing on appreciation

▶ Episode 4 – Rob Robson. Emotions and motivations during change.

▶ Episode 27 – Matt Fairbrass. Intuition versus logic in organizations.

▶ Episode 40 – Helena Clayton. Creating the space for love and connection at work.

Chapter 7
Storytelling

The final stage is to translate everything that we have learnt through the ChangeStories® ARIAS model into a story/ meaningful narrative that creates emotion and is authentic. This compelling change story will focus on outcomes and what it will look and feel like to work in the organization in the future.

If you have already completed the previous aspects of the ChangeStories® ARIAS model, you will have seen what a difference building these practices into your daily work can make. Hopefully, you will already have seen how these techniques improve engagement and understanding of change. This final stage is to bring together all the information that you now have about your organization and the change that you are facing into a really great story to share with others.

In the next section of this book, we will focus on building and performing this story, but here, we will focus on some story principles and activities to practise your storytelling capabilities:

- ▶ The characteristics of a compelling change story;
- ▶ Common story structures;
- ▶ Creating your own story.

The characteristics of a compelling change story

Ten years ago, I worked in an organization that had seven different change programmes going on, none of which communicated with each other or were joined up in any way. Every day, employees received multiple emails and messages relating to changes and it was impossible to see how they were connected. My role was to stitch together the different narratives about each of these change programmes into a compelling story so that employees could clearly understand what was changing and how they might be expected to work differently in the future. This was to ensure that employees were not being bombarded with multiple contradictory messages and could easily understand how their world at work was going to change in the future. Creating an overarching story for multiple change programmes is a really important activity that is often forgotten about, as individual change programmes focus on communicating about what they are doing without trying to stitch together some overall messages.

In undertaking this work, I thought about change programmes that I had experienced (both as an employee and as a consultant), how the key messages from these programmes had been communicated and how they had been received. I then used the themes that I identified from this process to think about the key characteristics of the change communications that had really worked, in the sense that they were well received by employees and got the message across that needed to be shared.

I discovered that in order for any communication about a change to be effective it needs to:

- Emphasize what is ending and what is beginning through the change process (as suggested by the Bridges transition model);

- Include evidence of how things of value from the past are going to be carried forward (as suggested by appreciative inquiry research);

- Clearly show that some things are remaining the same whilst other things are changing;

- Be built using storytelling principles such as status quo, conflict and/or adversity and elements of surprise, a turning point and then a resolution. There needs to be scene setting at the beginning so that people know they are hearing a story and there has to be context.

Earlier in the book, this idea of adversity in stories leading to emotion was discussed. Talking about adversity is important as this is what resonates with people and makes a story more authentic and believable. If we are truly going to create a meaningful and compelling story of change, it must acknowledge the good and the bad and acknowledge that there may well be difficult moments in the days ahead.

Common story structures

We've already discovered some of the structural elements of stories in earlier chapters. As a reminder, most stories include these elements:

- Scene setting;

- Something will go wrong (Mike Adams calls these conflicting factors in his book about business storytelling[1]);

- A turning point will be reached;

- The conflict will be resolved and success will follow.

Activity – Story structures in television, books and film

Think about your favourite film stories or origin stories about famous businesses that you might know of.

Note down the core elements of the film storyline or origin story. Chances are, they will follow the story structure as outlined above.

This story structure is common across so many cultures and it has even been said (although this may be apocryphal) that there are only two types of stories in the world – someone goes on a journey and a stranger comes into town. I'm not sure whether it is quite that simplistic, but it is true to say that so many stories that we find compelling follow this story arc.

To look at a change story example from the business and entertainment world, let's consider the story of Netflix. Remember Netflix started out as a DVD-by-post subscription service but when people could start streaming films because of better internet speeds, they had to adapt (otherwise they would be like Blockbuster – remember them?).

So, they decided to focus on streaming films even though people weren't sure what streaming really was. They had to persuade customers to act differently, so they told a story:

Sometimes it's hard to find a movie everyone can enjoy on a Friday night. For individuals and families with internet access, Netflix instantly streams an unlimited number of TV shows and movies, anytime, anywhere. Simply search, browse and watch on the easy-to-use website, mobile apps, apps on game platforms and hundreds of internet-connected devices. With one-click anyone can watch ad-free, HD quality, TV shows and movies. It's month-to-month and you can cancel anytime. We offer a one month free trial. Netflix, it's movie enjoyment made easy.[2]

I love this example of a change story:

- It's simple and easy to understand;

- There is some information setting the story in context but not so much that the story gets too complicated;

- The point of the story is explained;

- There is a clear explanation of what the future is going to look like;

- It creates emotion. In this case, it creates excitement at this future of unlimited possibilities of entertainment at the push of a button.

Now, of course, the world has moved on and most of us have unlimited entertainment possibilities at our fingertips. But consider how you might have felt if you had heard this story back in 2005 when the concept behind this story first started to take shape. It would have been so exciting and you would have wanted to be part of it.

This classic story structure can be found in many forms and another famous example is from Joseph Campbell's book, *The Hero's Journey*. In this story, a hero goes on a journey or quest. George Lucas was very influenced by this story form for *Star Wars*. The key stages of this story are:

- Introduction to the hero in the quest;

- The call to adventure;

- The hero is reluctant at first and has a fear of the unknown;

- The hero is encouraged by a wiser person;

- The hero passes the first threshold and fully enters the world of the new story;

- The hero encounters tests and helpers;

- The hero reaches the innermost cave;

- The hero endures the supreme challenge and emerges with a clearer sense of purpose and character;

- The hero takes possession of the treasure;

- The road back again and the chase;

- The hero returns with the treasure back to the ordinary world.

Now, this story is troubling for many as it emphasizes the 'leader as hero' narrative which can be negative for both organizations and individuals. This can also pressurize leaders into having all the answers, which as we have already discussed in this book is not helpful. In addition, change must be a collaborative effort in order to be successful. Therefore, *The Hero's Journey* is not necessarily a great fit for a successful change story. But, as it is a well-known story, I share it here as it may resonate with you.

A structure that I prefer is the Pixar Story Spine. You may also have heard of this structure, which is behind the success of many Pixar films. There are plenty of sources online to find out more about this structure,[3] but it is best illustrated through an example. Here I am using *The Wizard of Oz*:

- **Once upon a time** there was a little girl named Dorothy who was carried by tornado to the magical land of Oz.

- **Every day**, she journeyed toward the Emerald City in order to ask the Great and Powerful Wizard of Oz to help her get home.

- **But one day**, she got to Oz and she met the Wizard.

- **Because of that**, the Wizard told Dorothy that he would only help her get home if she killed the Wicked Witch of the West.

- **Because of that**, Dorothy encountered many dangers and was finally successful in destroying the witch.

- **Because of that**, the Wizard agreed to take Dorothy home in his hot-air balloon.

- **Until finally**, on the day of their departure, Dorothy ran after her dog, Toto, and missed the balloon.

- **And ever since then**, Dorothy learnt that she always had the power to get home on her own, which she did.

I often use the Pixar Story Spine, particularly when describing my own work when I meet people for the first time. I personally find it an easier structure to work with than *The Hero's Journey* when describing my own career.

Here's an example of the Story Spine applied to me:

Twenty years ago...

I worked in a Big Four consultancy, working on large change and transformation projects with different organizations across many different sectors. I loved my job! All my clients were keen to achieve change and it was exciting to work on these projects, but over time, I became aware that most of the projects didn't achieve what they set out to do and the process-driven approach to change often caused problems within the organizations such as reduced employee engagement.

Every day...

I saw leaders and managers trying to achieve change but without a clear blueprint for doing so. I saw employees becoming frustrated and fatigued by constant change. Myself and my colleagues worked long hours trying to push through change but sometimes people just didn't want to hear what we had to say. The approach that we were using just didn't seem to work. There seemed to be other factors that were impacting on the organizations and their ability to create change that our approaches just couldn't understand or reach.

I felt that there was a different way of managing change in organizations but I wasn't sure what it was.

Then one day...

A few years later, and now working for myself, I worked on a project where the organization concerned wanted to use storytelling as a means to create change. The top team in this organization learnt how to tell a story to share their future vision rather than simply reading from a set of slides. This approach led to much greater buy-in from employees into the new vision for change.

Because of that…

I realized that there might be a different approach to achieving change, and maybe storytelling and stories might be part of this. I realized that I needed to learn more about how this might work.

Because of that…

I decided to undertake some research into organizations going through change to see what factors impacted on their ability to create change. I also investigated how stories could be used in organizations to create change. This eventually led to me completing a PhD in organization change and storytelling.

Until finally…

After undertaking eight years of research, I discovered that there are a lot of hidden factors in organizations that impact on the ability to create sustainable change. I also discovered that telling and listening to stories from employees helps uncover what is important to them and can be used to drive successful change.

Now, I work with organizations to share what I have learnt and enable them to create more successful and long-lasting change which results in high levels of employee engagement, reduced costs and reduced timescales to achieve change.

I think that this is a far more compelling way to talk about my career journey than simply going through the different employers that I have had!

Why don't you have a go at using this structure to talk about your own journey to where you are now?

Creating your own story

Often when I am working with organizations and leaders to build their storytelling skills, it can feel daunting to immediately launch into creating a change story. So, a good place to start is to think about your own story, either as a leader or a change professional.

Writing and sharing your own leadership or career story is a great way to practise your storytelling skills – after all, you are creating a story about a subject matter that you know very well – as well as understanding more about yourself. I like to use the work of Noel Tichy and Ken Blanchard[4] here to shape a story.

Noel Tichy[5] has undertaken extensive research in this area and has determined that the most effective leaders have a clear point of view about themselves and the organization that they work in and are able to share it with others through a story. Ken Blanchard refers to this as a leadership point of view, 'your personal elevator pitch, your journey, your values, your goals and your expectations.'[6]

Often, we look to other leaders for inspirational stories, but it is also important to think about your own story and what you have learnt. This can be even more powerful to share with others than the story of a famous leader such as Jack Welch or Richard Branson.

Activity – Develop your story

To start developing your own story, ask yourself the following questions and make a note of your answers:

- Who are the influencers in your life who have had a positive (or negative) impact on your life and what did you learn from these people about leadership?

- Think about your life purpose. Why are you here and what do you want to accomplish?

- ▶ What are your core values that guide your behaviour? (Try to limit this to the 3–5 really core values)

- ▶ Given what you have learnt from your past experience and your purpose and values, what is your leadership point of view – your beliefs about leading and motivating people through change?

- ▶ What story would you tell to illustrate this?

You can also use a timeline to plot out your career to date to help you to think about the things that have happened to you that have made you who you are. This doesn't need to be anything complicated, just a simple timeline where you note down the key events.

Plot out your career experience to date on the timeline, noting the levels of enjoyment and achievement you have achieved at different points. You might also want to look back on these achievements with what you know now and see if there is anything you can learn about yourself that might help you think about your leadership story.

Bernadette Jiwa, in her book *Story Driven*, talks about the need to know the story of your business/yourself to make sure that you stand out. She emphasizes that it is important not to worry about differentiating yourself from the competition, just tell a real story.

It doesn't need to be the 'right' story, just something real and authentic.

Don't be afraid of showing who you really are.

Building storytelling into your daily practice

The next section of the book gets down into the detail of building your change story and creating your story is a really great place to start.

Here are some other storytelling exercises that you can try to strengthen your story muscles.

Writing a success story

Next time you are asked to write a case study about a piece of work that you have completed, you might want to think about taking a storytelling approach to this and write a success story instead.

Many organizations (my own included) like to share examples of their work and their successes to illustrate who they are as an organization and what they are like to work with. Mike Adams (in his excellent book *Seven Stories Every Salesperson Must Tell*) calls these 'success stories' or 'why should I work with you?' stories.

They require a slightly different approach to a traditional case study as in this, you (or the company that you work for) are the guide rather than the hero of the story. Thinking back to a more traditional case study, we've all seen the format of a customer with an issue that the company or individual solved for them. The focus here is different and is on how you guided the customer to their own success. The focus is not on the work that we did – the situation, the solution that we discovered and then the result.

Try asking yourself these questions and then formulate a few paragraphs of a success story in response:

- ▶ Who is the customer?

- ▶ What was their problem? How did they feel, what was the impact of it?

- How did they meet you as their guide? (Remember, you are Yoda, not Luke Skywalker)

- What was the plan that we made together?

- What were our concerns?

- How were these overcome?

- What did success look like when we got there?

- What did we learn that we would apply next time?

If you want to see some examples of success stories, take a look at my website where there are a variety of stories of work that I have completed in recent years.

Creating a story from a strategy document

If you have a strategy document that you want to make more engaging and interesting by applying storytelling principles, use these questions when thinking about what and how to communicate:

- What is most important to the recipient of my story? What are they interested in and what do they need to hear?

- Why am I sharing this story?

- What outcome and action do I want from sharing my story? What do I want to people to know, feel and do after receiving my story?

- What emotion do I want to create from my story?

You can then add more information to personalize the story and make it relevant to your audience (and to you):

- What am I excited about as a leader, in relation to this strategy?

▶ What am I worried about and what am I going to do to deal with these worries?

▶ What are my team going to be most excited/scared about in relation to this strategy?

Have a go at applying these principles to some of the words on your company website or the most recent strategy document. What difference does it make to how interesting and engaging the information is?

ChangeStories® podcast episodes focusing on storytelling

▶ Episode 2 – David Lee. The power of stories to communicate and create change.

▶ Episode 12 – Hamish Thompson. Making sense of storytelling in corporate communications.

▶ Episode 29 – Angus Fletcher. The science of storytelling, narrative and creativity.

▶ Episode 30 – Steve Bellis. The power of digital storytelling.

▶ Episode 36 – Scott McArthur. Why facts don't change minds but stories do – the importance of future literacy.

▶ Episode 38 – Vikki Kirby. The power of stories to drive change and encourage action.

PART III
BUILDING YOUR CHANGE STORY

I hope that by now you are raring to go and ready to start creating your own change story, especially now that you have developed your own individual story. You can use the ChangeStories® ARIAS model to gather the information that you need to create a compelling change story for your own organization or team and build engagement along the way. Each chapter of the previous section provided you with insights which you can use in this story, and the purpose of this final section of the book is to help you to craft this story, using a series of steps.

It can feel difficult to know where to begin when embarking on using stories for the first time. Individuals and teams that I have worked with have often said that they want guidance on how to shape and structure their stories and where to gather information from to inform their stories.

Sometimes people say that they are not entertaining enough or funny enough to be a good storyteller. Or they think that they are not creative enough to move away from their existing methods of communication. We will explore why each of these are simply not true as we move through the next chapters. But, many people are slightly fearful of using stories if they are not used to it. You may in fact be feeling that way yourself right now.

Have no fear. Many people that I work with feel the same and this next section was born as a solution. It gives you a simple guide to follow to help you to be the best storyteller that you can be.

Using this guide will enable you to:

> Take all the information that you have already gathered using ARIAS to act as inputs to your compelling change story;

> Find other sources of inspiration and information for your story that already exist within your organization and discover how to use them most effectively;

- ▷ Shape a compelling story in as little as 15 minutes (using a template that has been tested in multiple organizations and where I have seen this happen in practice!);

- ▷ Build and enhance the essential characteristics and behaviours that you need to become a confident story performer, whilst remaining authentic to your own style;

- ▷ Continue to review, reflect and enhance on your stories as you tell them so that every telling is as engaging as the first time, enabling you to build feedback and new information into your story as you go along.

There are four steps to consider:

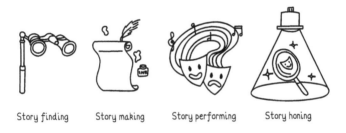

Story finding   Story making   Story performing   Story honing

As with the images used earlier in the book, these have been chosen to be memorable but also to represent something about what is required for each step.

Firstly, story finding is represented as a set of opera glasses, encouraging us to look deeply at both the information that we have discovered using ARIAS but also throughout our organization as we begin to build our story.

A pen and ink on paper is used to illustrate the process of story making as most stories, even if they are going to be verbal, will begin by being written out. And, to be honest, an image of a computer wouldn't look as nice as an old-fashioned quill and ink!

The third step, story performing, is illustrated with theatrical images and musical notes, highlighting the performative nature of telling your story.

And finally, the last step, story honing, is represented by a magnifying glass under a spotlight. It is important to continue to develop your stories, examining them carefully each time you tell them, to ensure that they continue to be relevant and authentic.

This next section walks you through each step of the process in detail:

Chapter 8 focuses on story finding and how you can use the information that you have already gathered using ARIAS to help shape your story;

Chapter 9 explains the story-making template that has been developed to make it easy to create your story and shows you how to use it to build your change story in as little as 15 minutes.

Chapter 10 focuses on story performing to enable you to feel more confident in your abilities as a storyteller, including considering performance and the characteristics of a story that is memorable for all the right reasons.

Finally, Chapter 11 gives tips for story honing – how to refine and reflect on your story every time that you tell it.

Let's start at the beginning, where do you find the content for your story?

Chapter 8
Story finding

Working through the different elements of the ChangeStories® ARIAS model will give you a wealth of information to use in your story. By paying attention to what you see and hear around you, reflecting on your own experiences, appreciating the best of what is in the organization and undertaking real inquiry in the organization, you should begin to notice themes and trends of what you are hearing and experiencing. These themes will tell you what is important to people and this is what you can focus on in your change story.

But there will be other sources of information available to you that already exist in the organization, and we will consider how to find and use these in this chapter:

- Finding story artefacts in your organization;

- Understanding the origin stories of your organization;

- The importance of nostalgia;

- Bringing this all together into your story.

Finding story artefacts in your organization

Going back to Schein's culture model, there are the visible artefacts that are all around us in the organization. For example, company reports, strategy presentations, company origin stories, photographs, all of which provide useful insights into what matters in the organization.

When I am working with a new organization, I pay real attention to what is around me as I wait to be collected by my host in the office reception.

- What photographs/pictures are on the wall?

- Are they of people, and if so, of whom?

- Are they images of nature/offices/landscapes?

- What do the choice of images tell me about what is important in this organization?

Spend some time wandering around your office or looking at the company website and intranet. What themes emerge for you from this and how can you use this in your own storytelling?

Artefacts in organizations can be surprisingly powerful. When I was still working in large consulting firms, the firm that I was working for was taken over by another. Many people who I worked with were very unhappy with this situation and this was compounded when, on the first day working for our new employer, some organization artefacts that we took for granted were changed. Now, these were minor things – the type of biscuits that were available in the meeting rooms and the type of toilet paper that was available – but they took on a major significance. The new biscuits and toilet paper were seen to be much cheaper than those which we had before and this led to bad feeling in the new employees, of which I was one.

What was this organization that we had become part of and why did they think so little of us? I'm sure there were good reasons for saving money on these seemingly unimportant items. And, on reflection, perhaps the previous biscuits had been rather extravagant! But by not paying attention to these small artefacts (and not communicating the need to change), there was an immediate negative impact on employee morale and productivity.

Understanding the origin stories of your organization

In organizations, history and the past are often brushed aside as something that is no longer important. But the history of an organization is a shared experience for employees and one which shapes how they feel about the organization and their role within it. Most organizations, even those who have only been around for a short while, have a rich history of stories, characters and previous change initiatives which can all impact on the success of any future change.

But, most organizations do not take the time to understand this history and the stories surrounding it when they embark on a change programme. This could be because most organizations are forward-looking rather than reflecting on the past. And yet, engaging with this history can have a very powerful impact on an organization's ability to create change.

If you think about most organizations, their history is made up of a series of stories or narratives. These might be stories about key figures in the organization or key events that have taken place. Many organizations have a foundation story that explains how they were formed and where they came from. Organizations such as Dyson[1] and 3M[2] use these stories to explain their key innovations and how they got to where they are now. These stories explain how the organizations got here but these tend to be fairly linear accounts and are not always used to illustrate what is important in the organization. When I think back to some of the presentations that I did to clients in the past, we spent a long time talking about all the clients that we had worked with and when we were formed but not much about who we were.

Often, this is as far as 'official' history stories of organizations go.

In reality, there are a lot of other history stories going on in organizations that are created by individuals rather than the organization as a whole.

As we know, we use stories in every part of our lives. Narratives and stories are an important tool that we as humans use to make sense of the past and to explain decisions and processes that are being made now and in the future. Reading a foundation story such as the examples above give a sense of what the organization is like. But it is only a snapshot of the organization and represents what the leaders and communication experts in the organizations actually 'want' us to know. However, the reality of life inside many organizations is that they do not conform with their official biographies. There are a lot of other stories being told by people in (and outside of) every organization that play just as much a part in how successful change can be.

I worked with a client recently who told me about a story they had heard about someone who had worked in the organization many years ago and what they would have thought about the changes that were being proposed. The person in the story had left many years ago and the people telling the story had never met them. However, this key person and their achievements continued to be an influence on the way things were done in this organization as their story continued to be told. This illustrates perfectly why these stories can really anchor an organization or a team in the past. Interestingly, if I had not been working with this organization to encourage storytelling, I wonder whether this story would ever have been unearthed?

Now, you might by now be thinking that unearthing these stories and finding the story that you want to tell seems like a lot of work. You wouldn't be wrong, but I hope you will see that this is a worthwhile effort to truly understand the organization and work with what already exists in the organization to create meaningful change. Engaging with stories requires effort as it involves excavating into the underneath parts of the organization. As Robert Macfarlane says in his wonderful book *Underland*, 'actively [retrieving] something from the underland almost always requires effortful work.'

Organizations are discovering that understanding more about their organization origin stories is important not just in a change context but also for leadership generally. Research reported in the *Harvard Business Review*[3] has shown that leaders can make use of key aspects of the past to pull people together towards a future common purpose. It reminds people of 'who we are' within an organization and creates stronger bonds between individuals. This links with the principles of appreciative inquiry which suggest that people are more likely to change in future if they feel that something from the past that they value remains consistent. But if we do not know what they value from the past, it is impossible to connect with it.

Leaders can make use of the historical organization stories in other ways too, particularly to create legitimacy and authenticity around future change plans by linking them back to these valued stories from the past.[4] There is a real strategic reason then for spending time understanding the history of the organization that is shown to us through origin stories and other stories from the past. It is more than just simply understanding what might get in the way of a change programme. Understanding the history, the stories that are told about it and how this might link to your future strategy can provide leaders with the tools that they need to drive more successful change in their organization.

As well as at an organization level, these history and origin stories are also relevant to the way that teams operate. Jon Harding, in his podcast conversation with me, shared his TRIBE (Tradition, Relevance, Identity, Belonging, Effectiveness) model, where the shared identity of the team is created through a number of factors, one of which is the traditions and history of the team. As well as other factors such as understanding the purpose and measures of effectiveness for the team, this history forms a core part of how the team sees themselves in relations to others in the organization. When creating change, it is important to consider organizational history on a number of levels. There are always 'a number of threads' that lead us to where we are now (a lovely phrase that Matt Fairbrass uses to describe organizational complexity in my podcast conversation with him) and we need to unpick these to understand more about our organization and our teams.

The importance of nostalgia

Stories about the past in organizations are often discounted as nostalgia trips on the part of employees, a return to a time when everything was golden. I would encourage you though to really listen next time you hear one of these nostalgic stories as they can be very illuminating. I see nostalgia as a barometer of what is important to people in organizations and this is a view shared by others in the organizational storytelling field, not least Yiannis Gabriel, one of the founders of this field of study.

In a series of fascinating articles,[5] Professor Gabriel examines the concept of nostalgia in organizations in depth and, in particular, highlights the importance and usefulness of examining nostalgia to make sense of what is important to individuals and groups in the organization. He says, '... the foci on which nostalgia fixates can give us deep insights into those elements of the present that cause discomfort, anxiety and distress, making nostalgia a useful instrument for the study of individuals and groups'.

Individuals in an organization who keep harking back to the past are considered to be blockers of change rather than individuals who can provide useful insights into the present. After all, as Professor Gabriel states, 'at a time when "innovation", "creative destruction" and "disruption" are lionized as universal virtues, mulling over the past seems decidedly passé'.

However, these thoughts of the past are certainly not negative and thinking nostalgically about the past, particularly about the good times, can increase motivation and can make it less likely that an employee will leave an organization. I have discovered that employees often tell nostalgic stories about the organization in which they work; remembering past experiences at work with great fondness. For many people, it is these memories that keep them in the organization. In one organization that I worked in, people often talked about the Breakfast Club that existed in the past, where everyone would meet up for breakfast together on a Friday. This had been lost as the organization grew in size but was something that was clearly valued. In my work with the leadership team of this organization, I encouraged them to think about ways of replicating this now, taking into account the larger scale of the organization. There might be stories like this in your organization too.

There is an opportunity here to link nostalgic thoughts of the past with hopes and dreams for the future. Thinking about the past as a group can have benefits such as bringing people together and creating a sense of togetherness in a team or organization. Therefore, undertaking work to discuss stories of the past as a group can be beneficial in both creating a sense of purpose and history and developing ideas for the future.

Appreciative inquiry suggests taking 'the best of what is' as a means of planning for future change.

Might nostalgia also help with this?

This would involve discussing what is valued and cherished from the past and then using this to build a platform for the future.

Bringing this all together into your story

To help you to find the story that you want to tell, I would encourage you to gather as much information as you can, based on your ARIAS outcomes and all the information that you have gathered from your study of organization artefacts and stories, both current and historical.

As you review this information, consider the themes that are emerging for you. These will indicate what is most important to people. I like to gather all the information that I have collected together (often on pieces of paper) and create mind maps or use Post-it notes to start grouping themes together. I can then move these themes around as I review more information.

You can test these themes with colleagues to see whether they resonate with them. Often, even when you think the information is disconnected, as you start to review it and work with it, a theme will leap out at you. I would suggest keeping to a limit of three key messages from your themes that you want to include from your findings. You can use more than this, of course, but it is advisable to keep to three key messages in each story as this is about the limit for human attention and concentration levels.

When working with existing content, particularly strategy documents and presentations, you may find that work is required to turn them into an engaging story. A lot of the work that I do with leaders in organizations is to assist them with this process. I'm sure we can all remember 'town hall' presentations where all staff are brought together to hear the latest updates and strategies from organization leaders. But can you actually remember what was said at these meetings? I suspect the answer to this is 'no' because these presentations – usually a series of PowerPoint slides, numbers and data – are presented because that is what the leadership team wanted us to know, rather than what we needed to know. Whilst the content of these presentations can be useful, I would urge caution in using them in their direct state, unless they are presented by a leader who is a skilled storyteller and has crafted their presentation in this way.

You now need to consider how you can present this information using stories to make it more engaging and how to decide what story you want to tell. When deciding what story you might want to tell, the starting point should always be to ask yourself a series of questions. You would usually begin with asking yourself what you want to share, but I would argue that starting from the perspective of the recipient of the story is always more valuable. Ask yourself:

> What is most important to the recipient of my story? What are they interested in and what do they need to

hear? (You can use the outputs of ARIAS for this as well as any other stories you have collected in your story finding)

▷ Why am I sharing this story? For information? To interest? To involve? To inspire?

▷ What outcome and action do I want from sharing my story?

▷ What do I want to people to know, think, feel and do after receiving my story?

▷ What emotion do I want to create from my story? (Remember emotion is key here – that is what makes stories memorable)

Phil Waknell,[6] a world expert in giving business presentations (and who has coached many leaders through their TED Talks), says that we need to focus on the transformation that we want to create when we share a presentation and/or a story. We will return to this later when we think about building excellent story-performing skills. However, at this stage, it is enough to think about the needs of the story recipient first rather than rushing straight into what you want to tell them.

It's also useful here to think about what could get in the way of your story being received in the way that it is intended. Firstly, knowing your audience is important and understanding what is most relevant to them. Then, it is about minimizing the opportunities for distractions away from your story. If you think about these in advance, you are more likely to be able to get your message across. Think about:

▷ Workloads and deadlines so that you can schedule a time to share your story which will minimize conflicts.

▷ Whether any of the information that you want to share in your story has been shared before. If it has been heard before, what was the response last time? Do you need to do anything differently next time?

▷ If you are sharing 'bad news', when is the best time to do this?

▷ Have there been any rumours about anything that you want to share in your story? How are you going to address these in the story?

▷ The words that you are going to use so that you can avoid technical language and words that your audience might not understand. Ideally, you should write your story down in the words that you would use to tell the story out loud. This avoids 'business speak' and will enable you to take a more conversational tone.

▷ How you are going to test the level of understanding of your story and engagement with it? Complex messages in particular may need more than one method of delivery plus opportunities for interaction so that you can check understanding and engagement with the message and also see whether perceptions and attitudes have changed as a result of your efforts.

▷ How you will reach people who might be out of the office on the day that you want to share your story.

▷ What channel is going to be best for sharing your story? There are a variety of options for either face-to-face, virtual or a combination of the two and making use of existing channels and methods is ideal.

Chapter 9
Story making

Earlier in the book, I shared a variety of story structures that exist, including the story arc, the Pixar Story Spine, *The Hero's Journey* and others. Based on my own experience of working with stories (and helping others to do the same), I have developed the ChangeStories® story-making template which will take you through a structured process to create your own story.

The structure is as shown in the following illustration. Each box represents a section of the story that you are going to create:

This structure has elements in common with the other story structures discussed in this book. There is an opportunity to set the scene at the beginning of the process; to share the outcomes of your ARIAS work and other story-finding artefacts that have gone into creating the story; a call to action and a clear picture of what the future will look like.

To help you with your story creation, you can download a template to start planning your story which contains a series of prompts and things to think about.

www.feldsparconsulting.com/changestories-the-book/

Let's work through the template in more detail now. This template has been used many times by me and also by my clients and one of the questions that I am most often asked is 'how long should my story be?'. The answer to that is 'it depends on what you want to use your story for'. Sorry, a typical management consultant answer, but let me explain further.

A written story can be longer than a spoken story. Ideally, a written story should be around one page of typed A4 paper and a spoken story should take you no more than 10 minutes to tell. But this is only guidance and you should be guided by what is going to work best for you as the storyteller and your audience. And also the time that you have available to tell your story. A short story is better than not using any story at all in my experience.

The final word on story length must go to the original writer on storytelling, Aristotle, who in his book *Poetics* says that even in the longest story, the recipient of the story must be able to keep the whole of the story in their mind, otherwise they will become lost and lose interest. An essential rule of thumb to keep in mind, I think!

Remember not to try and cram too much information into each story. Try to stick to three key messages in each story as this is about the limit for people to concentrate on. You could even have one key message and a number of supporting messages to provide additional context.

Let's work through how to use each section of the template.

We've discovered…

This is the beginning point of your story, setting the scene for who you are as an organization or team, what you have found out from your inquiry, conversations and story finding, what you have identified about what matters in the organization and what you would like to take forward into the future. Keep this section brief. It is simply to set the context for the story.

Questions to answer:

▶ Who are we as a team/organization?

▶ What makes us different?

▶ What do we value about our organization?

▶ How do we want to take this forward into the future?

Because of this…

Once you have set the context, you can then clearly state the issue that you have identified and why this needs to be resolved. This stage is often missed in change communications as so much focus is placed on 'selling' the change (advocacy) rather than inquiring about what problems need to be solved. Think back to the supermarket customer service analysis – you said, we did.

You can also refer back to the past again in this section, explaining why things that worked in the past are no longer suitable and why this change is now taking place.

Questions to answer:

▶ What is the issue or problem that needs to be solved?

▶ Why are things that we did in the past no longer working?

We are going to...

Here is your opportunity to explain clearly what is going to happen to resolve the issue. Keep it simple. There is a great piece of research by Anecdote[1] looking at retention of information and, unsurprisingly, information that is shared using simple language is more easily remembered and engaged with. As tempting as it is as a leader and/or a change professional to lapse into management or consultancy speak, keep it really simple here when explaining what is going to happen. No jargon or overly long words or flowery language. This is an important part of the story so it's worth spending time on both crafting the story and making sure that the messages that you want to impart are clearly understood.

Questions to answer:

> ▶ What are we going to do to solve the issue or problem?

> ▶ Who is going to help us with this?

> ▶ What have we already done to solve this problem?

So that...

This is another stage that is often missed when communicating a change and should include a discussion of why the change is needed and why now in particular. This is not a justification of the change, rather a chance to explain why this has to happen now, and what the consequences might be if that change doesn't happen. Some change models talk about creating a burning platform for the change and this is relevant here. But it is not about scaring people into accepting the change because of the dire consequences if they don't change. It is about explaining simply why the change has to happen and why it has to happen now. Again, this section doesn't need to be particularly detailed as it is all part of the context setting.

Questions to answer:

- Why do we need to change?
- Why now?
- What will the outcome be if we don't change?

And now...

This is the most important part of the story where you have the chance to really explain what the future is going to look and feel like, once the changes have been introduced. It is important to try and be creative here and evoke all of the senses of the people experiencing the story. What is their working day going to be like in this new world? What will they see, hear and touch in the future?

Think about this section from the perspective of the audience for the story. What are they going to be more interested in hearing about? What is in this for them? How will they benefit from this change? Ultimately, the question that most people are thinking about when they hear about something new is 'what's in it for me?'.

A client of mine was introducing new ways of working post Covid and was moving from a very traditional 5 days a week, in the office from 9am to 5pm culture to a much more fluid, flexible, work wherever you need to approach. This represented a major change to ways of working. To communicate this change, they decided to do away with the usual 'town hall' communication approach that they would have used in the past; instead, they decided to create a series of cartoons that illustrated how real-life employees would experience the new ways of working.

These cartoons, which were shared widely on the intranet and in team meetings, showed colleagues going about their day, sometimes working in the office, sometimes at home. They did a yoga class at lunchtime and then worked at the gym for the rest of the day. They got up early and worked from home, then went to a personal appointment, before heading into the office in the afternoon. The cartoons were engaging and created a lot of conversations about the change which ultimately led to greater acceptance of the future state as people really understood what it was going to be like.

Think back to large-scale communications that you have been at the receiving end of. What was most engaging for you and has lasted longest in your memory? It won't be a PowerPoint presentation of strategy slides but something that felt personal to you and that you experienced with all of your senses.

Questions to answer:

- What will the future look and feel like?
- What are the key change priorities?
- How do these link together and link to what we know about ourselves as an organization?
- What is in it for me (the listener/reader of the story)?
- What might be difficult during this process and how are we going to deal with that?

So you can...

The final stage of creating your story is to provide a place for people to go if they want more information. Thinking back to earlier discussions about resistance, what we perceive to be resistance is simply a lack of opportunity to ask questions. So, in the final section of your story you should signpost people to where they can get more information and support. You should also very clearly direct them to any actions that they need to take and also the timescales of what is going to happen next.

You can include any requests for help from the audience of your story here too. Is there anything that you need from them and how can they help? You can also share progress so far to achieve the change goal and how far there is to go.

At the end of the story, you want people to feel that they have the information that they need to process the change and also that the story reduces any feelings of uncertainty, lack of control and autonomy, as in the SCARF model (refer back to page 64 for a more detailed explanation of this model).

Questions to answer:

- ▷ What will happen next?

- ▷ What do I/my team need to do?

- ▷ Where can I get more information and support?

Whilst you might think it is easier to complete this template as an individual exercise, I have found that it works best when it is a collaborative effort. After all, change is a process that affects more than one person so it can be helpful to get different inputs into your change story before you use it for real.

Note that you do not have to use the 'we've discovered' headings if they don't work for your story. They are there to prompt and guide you and you should only use them if they feel authentic to what you are trying to say.

Worked example

To illustrate how this template works in practice, here is a completed example. This is based on a real project that I worked on but has been anonymized. In reality, it would contain a lot more information about the organization but that has been removed in this example. This represents an initial communication sent out to an insurance organization at the start of a major technology implementation project:

We've discovered...

Delighting our customers is at the heart of everything we do. It drives our behaviours and is what makes us different to our competitors. It is what brings our customers back to us year after year and is what makes employees join us and stay with us. This is who we are and this must continue into the future. It is important to all of us and is at our heart.

Because of this...

Unfortunately the systems in our customer contact centre are no longer fit for purpose. They have not been upgraded for some time and do not allow us to deliver the level of service that our customers deserve. Sometimes, we are unable to answer queries as promptly as we would like and there are examples of customers being sent the same information twice or having to repeat information on the telephone.

We are unable to respond to queries online so customers have to either call us or visit one of our branches. This does not reflect how our customers live their lives and we want them to be able to report claims or raise queries from their phones or via email.

The system issues are also frustrating for our customer contact centre colleagues. They are unable to deliver the level of service that they would like to and they are having to spend a lot of time moving between different screens and completing work off system.

We are going to...

We are going to focus on upgrading our systems so that they meet the needs of our customers and our customer contact centre teams. This includes a new technology platform and training for our customer contact centre teams and a major communications campaign to our customers.

We have undertaken a procurement exercise and engaged external consultants to support us through this process and have created an internal project team. We have already identified the system that we want to use as we believe this gives us what we need to move forward successfully.

We believe that the partners that we are working with will support us through this process of change, sharing our vision for change and enabling what we know is important about our organization to continue into the future.

So that...

We need to do this work now so that we can continue to deliver the level of service that our customers expect and to support our colleagues in the customer contact centre.

Whilst our customer retention rates remain high, our satisfaction ratings are falling and many customers state that the inefficiency of the current system is an issue.

We also know that our colleagues in the customer contact centre are finding the system difficult to use and this is impacting on their job satisfaction. This is evident from our most recent employee engagement survey results.

Our customer contact centres are at the front line of our customer experience and so it is essential that we have the best possible systems for our customers and for our colleagues.

And now...

In the future, our customer experience will improve with a seamless journey for the customer from starting their contact with us to when their issue is resolved. They will be able to contact us 24 hours a day, every day, in a way that works best for them and they won't have to telephone us or visit a branch if they don't want to. They will also be able to log in to an online system which will show the progress of their claim.

For our colleagues, there will be less transactional activity for them to complete off system as every aspect of their interaction with the customer will be system-based. The system will be quicker than currently and they will be able to clearly see tasks that they need to complete when they log in to the system at the start of their working day. There will be better guidance available in the system so that they can give the best possible advice and support to our customers.

All customer contact centre employees will receive training and support in the new system, tailored to their individual needs and requirements, to ensure that they feel comfortable using the system at go live. A full pilot and testing programme is planned prior to go live so that we know that everything works correctly.

For colleagues who do not work in customer-facing roles, there will be little to no change to how you work. You may notice more people in the office as the project team grows to support the change. We will continue to share progress with you and there will be opportunities to see the system in a series of roadshows and demos so that you can see what is changing.

We are excited about this project as it will enable us to bring our systems in line with industry standards and offer a much improved customer experience. Implementing new technology can be difficult but we have an excellent team around us who are supporting us through every step.

We are ensuring that we do not change what is already working well in our organization and that this will only be enhanced by the outcomes of this project.

So you can…

We will continue to share information about the project on the dedicated page on the intranet and in team briefings. Customer contact centre teams will be contacted individually by the project team to share more detailed information and to arrange for dedicated support through the change.

If you need more information, need support or have questions, please email the project team, go to the project pages on the intranet or discuss with your line manager.

This story was used at the very start of the project to communicate the future state and was accompanied by town hall briefings, briefings in team meetings and a dedicated intranet page which was regularly updated. The team continued to use and adapt the template to create stories throughout the project and the template and the stories were also shared with line managers so that they could adapt the content for their own teams.

This was the first time that this organization had used this approach to implement change, and at the end of the project it was felt by the leadership team that the different methods of communication had made implementation less painful and as a result there was little to no impact on levels of customer service throughout implementation.

There are lots more real-life examples of change stories, from a wide variety of organizations, available on the ChangeStories® website, so take a look for more inspiration.

www.feldsparconsulting.com/changestories-the-book/

The next time that you need to create a change communication, try using this template to craft the content. The structure helps to shape your thinking and focuses on the information that your audience are most interested in. It also enables you to capture these key elements quickly, then share them with others to get their input as it is useful to engage other people in the process of story creation.

Lessons learnt from using this template

There are a number of lessons that I have learnt from using this template in a variety of organizations:

- ▷ Create stories throughout a change process, updating the information each time, and share them constantly throughout the change;

- ▷ Roll up individual change programme stories into an overarching narrative which covers all change activity in the organization;

- ▷ You can never overcommunicate during a period of change, to ensure that you reach everyone. So, tell the story constantly, in as many different ways as you can, particularly focusing on oral storytelling. Introduce the key messages from the story into everyday communications and conversations;

- ▷ Share with line managers regularly and enable them to add their own anecdotes and content to the story to make it relevant and personal to their team;

- ▷ Involve as many people as possible in the creation of your story, to capture different perspectives and test your content;

- ▷ Stories should be flexible and adaptable and continually change to reflect what is going on in the organization at that moment.

Good luck and enjoy the process of story making.

In the next chapter, we will focus on building skills in telling stories to groups. Sharing stories orally is more effective than sharing written stories but is the part of using stories that leaders and change professionals find most scary. The next chapter will guide you through the process of telling a compelling change story.

Chapter 10
Story performing

Many leaders that I work with are concerned that they are not natural storytellers and that they simply won't be able to do it. Building stories into your practice is not about becoming a stand-up comedian or a raconteur if that doesn't come naturally to you. It is simply about telling a story in a way that is authentic to you and using the principles of storytelling and performance in your communications to build engagement.

I've mentioned Phil Waknell already and his work in creating engaging and transforming business presentations. I would highly recommend watching his TED Talk as it gives such great insight into how to feel more comfortable with presenting and communicating to groups. He talks about creating transformation in the audience which, as has already been discussed, is really important. He also came onto the ChangeStories® podcast and talked through his approach to presenting in episode 19.[1] Definitely worth a listen! One of the key lessons that I took from our conversation was that authenticity is key to bringing out your individuality. Phil said 'don't aim for perfection, aim for connection', which really stuck with me.

A key part of building stories into your practice is being personal and authentic, showing up as your true self and sharing stories of your personal experiences that add colour and interest to your presentations, as well as using storytelling principles in your communications. A part of this is also being prepared to be vulnerable. It's easier sometimes to hide behind a prepared PowerPoint slide deck rather than speaking from the heart. But, if you want to create true engagement with change, it is necessary to bring more of yourself to communications, and storytelling is a great way to do this.

Let's think about the characteristics of a well-told story. We can all think about times when we have been engaged by someone's communication style (and times when we have not). In my own experience, well-told and memorable stories share a number of characteristics:

- Easy to understand, coherent, well structured and well rehearsed;

- Authentic to the person telling the story;

- Strong physical presence and good use of voice;

- Told with humility;

- Create rapport and engagement.

A well-told story is easy to understand, coherent, well structured and flows from one section to the next. Having a structure or template to follow (such as the ChangeStories® story-making template) really helps here. It's important to practise your story so that you can link it together coherently before you tell it for the first time.

The story should be authentic to the person who is telling it and drawn from their own experiences. There is nothing wrong with using stories that you have heard from others but you should make it clear that that is the case. I did hear an example where someone told a story on stage at a conference, claiming it had happened to them. However, the person who actually was the original storyteller was in the audience and stood up, shouting at the person on stage that they were a liar! Not a good way to tell a story.

Whatever story that you tell should feel genuine to you as the storyteller, connecting with your values and weaving your personal experiences throughout.

Physical presence and use of voice is important in storytelling but should also be authentic to you as the storyteller. Again, practice is key here to build confidence and presence. We will cover this in more detail later in this chapter.

Finally, the story should be told with a sense of humility. Don't be tempted to only focus on good news all of the time as this makes a story less believable. Also, be prepared to give others the chance to share their stories and anecdotes as you tell your own story. A sure sign of an enjoyable and engaging story is when others want to join in too, so make sure that you leave some space to do this during or at the end of your story. It's worth noting here the difference between a story and an anecdote. An anecdote is a short description of a particular incident that illustrates a particular point. It is usually shorter than a story but is also a useful tool to add colour to any communication that you want to give. It can be a great way to hook people into your story at the beginning and make them want to hear more.

The well-told story enables the building of rapport through generating emotion/feelings and the sharing of beliefs and attitudes rather than simply sharing facts and information. There needs to be enough detail in your story to fully engage people and leave them wanting to find out more. Shawn Callahan[2] has developed a great set of criteria for a compelling story such as including something unanticipated, is relevant and relatable (similar to others' experiences), contains enough detail to enable people to visualize what happened, creates emotion and generates a desire to find out what happens next.

Peter Guber, writing in the *Harvard Business Review*,[3] explains that a story should have four truths in order to engage and move the audience:

▶ Truth to the storyteller – the storyteller is being authentic and honest in their storytelling;

▶ Truth to the audience – the storyteller provides opportunity for the audience to interact with and participate in the story, respects their time and fulfils any expectations that the audience might have;

▶ Truth to the moment – the storyteller intensively prepares their story but never tells it in the same way twice, reacting to each unique storytelling experience. They know that the context in which they are telling their story is essential and they tailor the story accordingly. It's back to the 'plan tight, hang loose' methodology of appreciative inquiry;

▶ Truth to the mission – the storyteller really believes in their story and why they are telling it and this is clear to everyone who hears their story. This passion evokes emotion and action in those who hear the story.

So, practice and preparation is important but so is reacting in the moment to the context. It is more important to be authentic and create connection than sharing the 'perfect' story. Focusing on these truths as you prepare to tell a story is a helpful way of ensuring that your story is as engaging as possible. In addition, this chapter is about you – the storyteller – and building your skills and confidence, by working on the following:

▸ Performing your story;

▸ Visual and data storytelling;

▸ Collaborative storytelling.

Performing your story

The idea of performing a story can feel intimidating and out of many people's comfort zone. But performance is important and can affect how your story is received. This is not about turning yourself into something you are not, it is simply thinking through some of the things that can get in the way of your story, particularly when you are delivering a story verbally. The main things to think about are:

▸ Body;

▸ Voice;

▸ Delivery.

Body

Your body language and facial expression needs to fit with the story that you are telling, and if it is in conflict this can be confusing and distracting for your audience. For example, telling a funny story with a frown on your face or telling a serious story whilst smiling throughout is not congruent. The aim is for your body language and facial expressions to be congruent to your story. Therefore, there is a need for a level of self-awareness here so that you know what your body is doing whilst you are speaking.

If this is difficult for you, try getting some feedback from a trusted person whilst you practice your story so that you can identify areas where your body language is not congruent with your story. Many of us aren't aware of what we are doing whilst we are talking so this is an important thing to increase awareness of. You could also video yourself whilst practising and notice your body language. This might be an uncomfortable experience but will definitely be illuminating!

Other aspects to consider are similar to those for other forms of communications or presenting. You can reduce distractions for the audience by limiting the amount that you repetitively move around whilst talking and also reducing 'fiddling' with coins/pens etc. This doesn't mean standing still whilst talking as being expressive is engaging but it is about reducing distracting, repetitive movement to a minimum. Again, getting feedback from others or from a video of you talking is great here to identify areas to work on.

Finally, maintaining eye contact with your audience is essential to create connection and engagement. Try to move your eyes around the room as much as you can so that everyone feels engaged.

Voice

Your voice is your most important tool when storytelling. Consider the volume of your voice, the tone that you are using and your pitch. The volume of your voice is the loudness (or softness) of your voice whilst pitch is the highness (or lowness) of your voice. Tone is the mood that you are conveying in your voice. The tone of your voice should be congruent with the story that you are delivering but you can vary volume and pitch throughout your story to maintain interest and draw people in. You can speak more loudly to emphasize certain points and use quieter speech to draw people into your story and create a more intimate environment.

Try playing around with different forms of volume and pitch as you develop your story, always aiming to keep within your natural range. As with most aspects of performance, practice makes perfect and regularly practising using your voice will help you to determine what works best for you. Watching TED Talks is a useful way to get ideas from other presenters. Observe when a presenter really draws you into their talk – how are they using their voice? What techniques can you learn from these observations?

You will be able to better control your voice if you are able to control your breathing so, if speaking in public makes you nervous, try some deep breathing exercises beforehand to calm your nerves and steady your voice. You will be more able to use the volume, pitch and tone of voice that you want to if your breathing is steady.

Delivery

Talking clearly and concisely, using normal everyday words, is key to delivering an engaging story. Try to speak at a normal speed and pause regularly to allow the audience to reflect and consider important points. Many people are afraid of silence when they are storytelling and yet it can be such a powerful communication tool as well as giving you time to think about what you might want to say next.

TED Talks are another useful tool here to think about your own delivery. Pay particular attention to the way that people start and finish their presentations and see if there are ways that you can use these in your own practice.

This is not a book about presentation skills so this is a brief overview of some of the areas to think about when you are preparing to tell your story. There is a wealth of information out there about public speaking and improving your skills. I would particularly recommend Ideas on Stage who have created a comprehensive guide which is available on their website[4] if you want to explore this further.

The important thing to remember is to be yourself! Review and get feedback on how you tell your story so that you can be the best you can be but also embrace your own quirks and individual ways of communicating. Your audience will feel far more engaged if they feel that they are experiencing you as you really are.

Visual and data storytelling

When thinking about how you want to tell your story, you might leap towards creating a presentation in PowerPoint as this may be your default mode for communicating verbally and is what feels safe and unscary. As Garr Reynolds says in his excellent book *Presentation Zen:*[5]

Fear is the path to the dark side. Fear leads to bullet points. Bullet points lead to boredom. And boredom leads to suffering.

I would strongly discourage you from leaping straight to creating a slide deck when using stories as there is plenty of evidence that excessive use of PowerPoint actually alienates an audience from the message that a presenter is trying to deliver. A well-delivered story without PowerPoint will be far more effective than an averagely delivered story accompanied by a slide deck.

That being said, the well thought through use of visuals can really add to your story. Powerful visuals to understand and remember can really add to a story but this is not 'death by PowerPoint'.

Garr Reynolds' book contains lots of great examples of fantastic visual storytelling, and also examples of where things don't work quite as well. Reading this book has really changed how I use PowerPoint and images in my communication.

Reynolds takes inspiration from the principles of zen living in Japan into the use of visuals in communication and encourages us to follow three simple principles when using visual imagery in our storytelling:

- Restriction – think about the story that you want to tell through images (and data) and use these images sparingly and thoughtfully;

- Simplicity – keep things as simple and clear as possible and avoid using too many colours and images;

- Naturalness – be natural in how you use visual elements in your delivery, and if your audience is not going to understand your visuals in a few seconds get rid of the visuals.

The best way to use engaging visuals in your story is to follow the principles above and really plan out in advance what visuals you are going to use. I like to do this planning away from a computer, thinking about the key themes that I am going to use in my story and then identifying images that I could use to support these themes. By doing this offline, often on bits of paper or Post-it notes, I can move things around in my presentation before then creating the visuals in PowerPoint. Develop the content of your story first and then identify the visuals that you want to use, rather than the other way round.

As well as using visuals to support your story, you can also use other media to communicate. I've already shared the example from a client of mine when they used cartoons to explain new ways of working to their teams. There is also really exciting work being undertaken in the field of digital storytelling, using film and other media to create engaging stories. I attended the 10th International Digital Storytelling conference at Loughborough University in 2022 and met Steve Bellis who later shared his expertise in an episode of the ChangeStories® podcast. He uses digital storytelling to support people to tell their own stories and has experienced the power of this process of storytelling. He shares his step-by-step guide to creating a digital story on the podcast and some of his own stories which I found very powerful and moving, both in the words that he chose to use and the images. Definitely worth a listen if you want to create something different in your storytelling.

In my conversation with Jennie Holyoake, we discussed data storytelling and how important it is to give a voice to numbers and data as they cannot speak for themselves. If you want to use data in your story, consider how you can present it to enable your audience to engage with it in a meaningful way. Usually, data is exposed in a presentation whereby it is simply presented as a table or financial statement. However, it is far more engaging to enable the audience to do more than this with data. Gramener, a leading data storytelling agency, use the following steps, where an individual will become increasingly engaged with the data as they move through the steps:[6]

- Expose – provide a simple financial statement or table of the data;

- Exhibit – provide a visual means to give a narration to the data, for example through a chart or diagram;

- Explain – provide a verbal explanation of what the data means;

- Explore – provide a means for the audience to play and experiment with the data.

Try this yourself next time you have to present some data to others and see if people are more engaged with the content.

Collaborative storytelling

So far, this chapter has focused on the individual skills that you need to build to hone your craft. This is important, of course, but this book is also about collaboration and engagement so it is useful to consider how to collaborate to create a shared story.

Collaborative storytelling can take many forms, from writing stories as a group to telling stories verbally around a campfire (real or imaginary, but there is something very powerful about sitting together around a real campfire!). At its heart is a process whereby multiple storytellers work together to build a story. It is a great way to learn from others, practise your skills, build in different perspectives and create a story that is going to engage and excite the maximum number of people.

Collaborative storytelling can take a variety of forms:

> Each person takes responsibility for writing a section of the story which is then combined together into a single story;

> A story is written together, in real time, similar to the writers' room method taken on many comedy television shows;

> One person writes the story but this is shared with others to get feedback and input.

Collaborative written storytelling is probably the easiest place to start and there is something wonderful about a group of people working together to create a shared outcome. A great place to start is where each person creates a section of the story which is then shared, feedback is given and the elements then combined together into a single story. The next chapter, story honing, has suggestions for asking for and giving feedback on a story which you could use as part of this feedback process.

Creating a story together in real time can take longer but is a very collaborative process. My favourite way of doing this is to use the story-making template key headings, on flipcharts or whiteboards around a room. Then, everyone in the room can suggest content themes to go under each heading. I usually get people to write each theme on a separate Post-it note and put them under the headings. Give people some time to do this and then start grouping the Post-it notes into themes. You can then repeat the process using the themes, with content being suggested under each theme on Post-it notes. You can keep repeating the process until the content has been honed down to the minimum elements of content that deliver the maximum outcome. It is then simply a matter of joining each of the elements together to create a coherent story. You can do this in the room as a collaborative process or one person can do this and then share the story for comment to the group. The writers' room process can be repeated each time you want to create a new story and also to discuss the outcome and feedback on stories once they have been shared.

Collaborative oral storytelling can be conducted indoors or outdoors and often involves sitting in a circle, sharing stories. There is a great power in speaking from the heart in this way but the vulnerability that is required does mean that the people involved in the storytelling have to be comfortable with each other and the group has to be well facilitated. Pelin Turgut[7] writes about the power of the circle and the process of listening, reflecting and building a shared story that takes place. It can be an amazing process to be part of but must be conducted in an environment of trust, openness and psychological safety.

Story circles have a rich history, often linked to the traditions of indigenous peoples around the world.[8] It is a simple process where people sit in a circle and share stories, often on a theme, but sometimes sharing whatever they feel in the moment. As each person shares their story, themes materialize, and at the end of the story circle a rich and complex story often emerges.

A typical story circle has up to 10 participants, with a facilitator to guide the process and take notes (if appropriate). The facilitator will usually start the process by telling a story that relates to a prompt question and then each participant will share their own story in turn. Participants pay full attention to each other when they are telling their stories (and try not to think about preparing their own stories!) and then move onto the next story without comment or discussion until everyone has had a turn to tell their story. There is no need for participants to prepare their stories in advance, they will emerge in the moment.

Example prompts that I have used in organizations for story circles include:

- Share a story which illustrates what it really feels like to work here right now;

- Share a story which explains why you joined this organization;

- Share a story about a time when you really felt you belonged in this organization;

- Share a story about a time at work which made you smile.

You could also use any of the reflective questions throughout this book as a prompt for your own story circle.

Story circles can be used with employees at different levels in organizations and can be a great activity to carry out within a team, if the conditions are right for people to speak honestly and truthfully. It can be useful to have a facilitator who is not part of the team, for example a member of your training team or an external facilitator. You can use this process to gather themes for your story or to develop a story together. I like to use it as a way to gather stories from people in an organization that I can then take away and develop into a story which I then share with them for feedback.

You've now built your story and developed your skills in storytelling, and you may even have had a go at telling your first story. I hope it went really well and you could see the difference that it made in the way that your message was understood and engaged with by the audience.

What next?

Well, storytelling is an iterative process and so you need to continue reviewing and developing your story to make sure that it adapts to the changing environment in your organization. We now move onto the final stage, story honing, which will enable you to do just this.

Chapter 11
Story honing

Storytelling should always be a reflective, iterative and ongoing process. A process of continual development and refinement so that the story is as good as it can be. This should include:

- Getting feedback on your story;

- Spotting more stories to include in your story repertoire;

- Creating a story bank.

Getting feedback on your story

Once you have created your story, you can then start to test it out and get some feedback on it. Start small by sharing your story with a few trusted colleagues or friends and ask them to give you feedback. For example:

- Was it interesting?

- What did they find most exciting?

- Could they see the key story elements in it?
  - A beginning, middle and an end
  - Characters
  - A plot
  - A sequence of events in time and space

- Once the story had finished, were they left with any questions?

- What else would they have liked to know?

- How was the delivery of the story?
  - Body
  - Voice
  - Delivery

- Did the story feel authentic to you, the storyteller based on what they know of you?

- How did they feel at the end of the story?

You can also observe the group whilst you are telling the story (or ask someone else to do this for you if you don't feel confident about telling a story and observing the room at the same time). Check the body language of the people you are telling the story to:

- How do they react during their story?

  - Posture

  - Eye contact

  - Facial expressions

- How do they respond to key elements in the story? For example, do they laugh/smile when you thought they would?

It's also useful to reflect on how you felt whilst you were telling your story:

- Did you feel comfortable/uncomfortable?

- How was the speed of your delivery? Did you feel that you were talking too fast or too slow?

- Did you remember every part of your story? Did you have to use notes?

Every time you tell a story, take some time to reflect afterwards on how it went and how you could make it even better next time.

Thinking about the principles of action learning, you could ask yourself the following questions as part of your reflective process:

- What happened when you told the story?

- How do you feel?

- What went well?

- What went less well?

- Why didn't it go so well?

- What do you need to do now?

- What are your next steps?

Spotting more stories

Once you start becoming more familiar with stories, you will start to see them everywhere, many of which you can use as part of your own toolkit. You can get even better at finding stories if you start being more aware of stories that you see or hear. A great way to practise your story-spotting skills is to take a look at www.thestorytest.com. There you can read extracts from company websites and reports and see whether they are stories or not – it's good fun. As we have seen, not all accounts are stories and whilst many organizations might say that they are using stories to communicate, in practice you will find that many are not. You can use Story Test to check out your knowledge of story structures so that you can tell when you see a story and when it is something else. The more you practise hearing and gathering stories, the better you will get at telling them.

Watching other people tell stories is also a great way to hone your own storytelling abilities. In particular, pay attention to beginnings and endings of stories. Starting and ending a story does take practice and it can be useful to observe how people get into and get out of their stories. You can then think about adding these skills into your own approach.

When I am telling stories, I tend not to start my stories with 'let me tell you a story' as this can feel a bit childish, as though I am reading a bedtime story! Instead, think of a great hook that you can use to get people interested in what you are going to say. In his TED Talk, Pixar writer Andrew Stanton[1] explains the use of a hook as a way to get the audience interested in your story by making them work a little, and this is what an audience want to do, although they don't necessarily want to know that they are doing that. They don't want you to explain everything to them. A bit of work on their part is what keeps them interested.

I often find this with films. If there is a lot of exposition at the beginning I get bored, whereas if I have to work a bit harder to understand what is going on my interest is maintained for longer. It's one of the reasons why I like the films by Christopher Nolan. I know others feels the same. He treats the audience as intelligent consumers of the film and enables them to find things out for themselves.

You can also think about how you want to end your story in an engaging way. Thinking back to the previous discussion about creating a transformation in your audience, what do you want them to do as a result of hearing your story? Can you tell them this as a way to end your story rather than simply petering out and saying 'well, that's it!' This is one of the key differences between business storytelling and the more classical storytelling forms. You are telling your story for a reason and your story has a point, in that you want to inspire action. So, let people know what this action is at the end of your story so that they know what to do next. The story-making template includes this specific element so that every story that you tell includes this very important aspect.

As you spot more stories, focus on the stories that are told and how they make you feel.

▶ What really interested you about the story?

▶ And did anything really make you disengage?

▶ What can you take from this into your own storytelling practice?

Creating a story bank

If you are trying to get into the habit of telling more stories as well as crafting stories for specific occasions, you want to have stories at hand whenever you want to emphasize a point or communicate something.

My storytelling colleague and friend David Lee told me about his own practice in this area, where he creates a story bank that he can draw upon at any time to find an appropriate story for every occasion. Whenever he experiences something that he thinks would be useful, he adds it to his story database, along with some keywords that he can search for, so that he has dozens of wonderful stories at his fingertips.

On his recommendation, I have done the same, creating a simple table in a Word document with the story outlined in one column and then a series of searchable key words in another. It really works and means that I don't have to try and remember lots of different stories.

Chapter 12
Concluding this story and taking action

We've covered a lot of ground in this book and I really hope that it has left you with a feeling of excitement and desire to introduce the power of storytelling, conversation and inquiry in your change management practice.

I know that when I first discovered the power of these tools, it transformed my way of working. In fact, it transformed my life as I now do completely different work to what I was doing 20 years ago and this has led me to write this book.

I hope that reading this book will also transform your everyday change management practice, and in fact your everyday leadership practice. So, to finish the story with an action, the next action for you to take is to decide how you are going take forward what you have learnt.

> ▶ Can you think of a time in the next few weeks when you can tell a story?

▶ How can you start to ask more questions and create more conversations in your organization?

▶ How can you build time for reflection into your day?

You can review your responses to the reflective questions throughout the book to create an action plan to take forward into the future.

▶ Were there particular chapters or areas of content that felt particularly challenging for you?

▶ Are there things that you are already doing that you can do more of in the future?

Know that things may not go perfectly at the beginning as you start to develop your skills. Even the most accomplished storytellers don't get it right every time. But, in my experience, it is better to tell an unpolished story than not tell a story at all. Obviously, if you are wanting to tell a story in a formal context, it is important for it to be as well practised and polished as possible, but if you have simply used more of the principles in this book in your everyday work, you will already see the benefits.

Tell people that you are experimenting with some new tools and ask for their feedback to improve your practice.

Continue to search for stories and inspiration wherever you can find it and learn from the way that others, perhaps more experienced storytellers, use the principles in this book.

I would recommend creating a plan so that you have a clear path to take as you start (or continue) your ChangeStories® journey. This can then guide you and give you something to reflect upon to see your progress. You can also share your plan with others so that they can support you in this journey.

Activity – ChangeStories® action plan

My goal is (write it in the present tense)...

Set a deadline for this goal...

My plan for achieving this goal is (list key tasks and timescales)...

The reasons that I want to achieve this goal are...

The ways that others can help me are...

I will know if my plan is working if...

Some things that could interfere with my plan are...

If my plan isn't working, I will...

I need to learn and develop the following to achieve my goal...

Finally, don't forget that at heart, we are all storytellers and it is something intrinsic in us.

We are all curious and enjoy asking questions and having stimulating and interesting conversations.

Sometimes, we just forget how and when to do this as we grow up.

So, my advice to you is to just do it!

Build storytelling, conversation and inquiry into your daily life as often as you can.

Keep it simple and practise.

And most of all, enjoy it!

About the author

Dr Susanne Evans is an organization change consultant and researcher on a mission to change the way that transformations are managed. Having spent 10 years in Big 4 consultancy firms, she saw first-hand how difficult it was to achieve the benefits of large-scale transformation programmes.

Her PhD research focused on the role of stories in transformation and she distilled both this research and her 27 years of hands-on consultancy experience to create the ChangeStories® approach, enabling her clients to use stories, ask questions and have powerful conversations to drive change.

As well as writing and speaking regularly for platforms such as the Change Management Institute, Business Transformation Network and APMG, Susanne hosts open storytelling workshops, supporting people in writing a compelling story for themselves.

She is the also the host of the highly rated ChangeStories® podcast, in which guests share ideas for improving the way that changes are managed in organizations.

Susanne loves swimming, food, travel and archaeology and is inspired by all of these in her work.

To find out more, visit www.feldsparconsulting.com

Endnotes

Introduction

[1] https://hbr.org/2003/06/storytelling-that-moves-people

Chapter 1: The history (and reality) of change management in organizations

[1] www.emerald.com/insight/content/doi/10.1108/JOCM-06-2015-0089/full/html
[2] www.tandfonline.com/doi/full/10.1080/14697017.2011.630506#.UiR-ZbwmwfE
[3] hbr.org/2000/05/cracking-the-code-of-change
[4] www.youtube.com/watch?v=fzgdduGx81E
[5] www.ekrfoundation.org/5-stages-of-grief/change-curve/
[6] https://timharford.com/books/messy/
[7] https://wmbridges.com/about/what-is-transition/
[8] https://neuroleadership.com/your-brain-at-work-the-book/
[9] https://hbr.org/2017/08/high-performing-teams-need-psychological-safety-heres-how-to-create-it
[10] https://mitsloan.mit.edu/ideas-made-to-matter/5-enduring-management-ideas-mit-sloans-edgar-schein
[11] https://psycnet.apa.org/record/2017-22409-005
[12] https://link.springer.com/chapter/10.1057/9780230277953_15

Chapter 2: Leading change differently using stories

1 Sources: Noel Tichy, 'The Leadership Engine'; McKinsey & Company, 'Change Leader, Change Thyself' and 'Developing Better Change Leaders'; Erica Ariel Fox, 'Winning from Within'.
2 www.researchgate.net/publication/228631134_Building_trust_in_ times_of_crisis_Storytelling_and_change_communication_in_an_airline_ company
3 https://journals.sagepub.com/doi/10.1177/1350508414527248
4 www.taylorfrancis.com/books/edit/10.4324/9780203471005/lines-narrative-norman-denzin-amal-treacher-corinne-squire-molly-andrews-shelley-day-sclater
5 https://hbr.org/2014/10/why-your-brain-loves-good-storytelling
6 https://significantobjects.com
7 https://pubmed.ncbi.nlm.nih.gov/20660768/
8 http://wiredforstory.com/story-genius-1
9 https://uk.sagepub.com/en-gb/eur/narrative-methods-for-organizational-communication-research/book209826
10 www.gsb.stanford.edu/insights/jennifer-aaker-seven-deadly-sins-storytelling
11 www.anecdote.com/2015/01/link-between-memory-and-stories/

Chapter 3: Attention

1 https://journals.sagepub.com/doi/abs/10.1177/1548051816664681
2 www.tandfonline.com/doi/abs/10.1080/14697017.2017.1299370? journalCode=rjcm20&
3 www.sciencedaily.com/releases/2013/10/131030111345.htm
4 https://hbr.org/2015/01/the-authenticity-paradox
5 https://hbswk.hbs.edu/item/the-truth-about-authentic-leaders
6 www.linkedin.com/pulse/my-response-adam-grants-new-york-times-oped-unless-youre-brené-brown
7 www.sciencedaily.com/releases/2013/10/131030111345.htm
8 www.charlesduhigg.com/the-power-of-habit
9 www.timetothink.com
10 https://hbr.org/2016/10/leaders-who-get-change-right-know-how-to-listen

Chapter 4: Reflection

[1] https://sloanreview.mit.edu/article/learning-when-to-stop-momentum/
[2] https://calnewport.com/knowledge-workers-are-bad-at-working-and-heres-what-to-do-about-it/

Chapter 5: Inquiry

[1] https://flora.insead.edu/fichiersti_wp/inseadwp2003/2003-92.pdf
[2] https://journals.sagepub.com/doi/10.1177/017084069501600305
[3] https://leandroherrero.com/some-companies-are-run-as-a-permanent-focus-group-2/
[4] https://hbr.org/2019/08/learning-is-supposed-to-feel-uncomfortable
[5] www.cairn.info/revue-management-2013-5-page-653.htm
[6] www.hult.edu/blog/the-coaching-leader-food-for-life/
[7] www.linkedin.com/pulse/remembering-jane-magruder-watkins-how-she-lived-her-dash-mckenna
[8] https://amycedmondson.com/psychological-safety/
[9] www.gallup.com/workplace/236198/create-culture-psychological-safety.aspx
[10] https://orca.cardiff.ac.uk/id/eprint/101129/1/Resistance%20Redux_Final.pdf
[11] https://journals.sagepub.com/doi/abs/10.1177/0170840616685360?journalCode=ossa
[12] www.researchgate.net/publication/211386189_I_am_not_your_hero_Change_management_and_culture_shocks_in_a_public_sector_corporation
[13] https://journals.sagepub.com/doi/10.1177/0170840617717554
[14] www.ted.com/talks/chimamanda_ngozi_adichie_the_danger_of_a_single_story?language=en
[15] https://hbr.org/2005/05/your-companys-secret-change-agents
[16] https://cathbishop.com/the-long-win/
[17] https://humannatureatwork.com/wp-content/uploads/2017/06/Courageous-Conversations-That-Work-4-components-must-get-right.pdf

Chapter 6: Appreciation

[1] www.researchgate.net/publication/265225217_Appreciative_Inquiry_in_Organizational_Life

[2] https://journals.sagepub.com/doi/full/10.1177/0021886320936265

[3] www.semanticscholar.org/paper/Language-of-Life-Giving-Connection%3A-The-Emotional-Robson/020a0c669cded4927e7deef38eacf46b6f6bd160

Chapter 7: Storytelling

[1] www.youtube.com/watch?v=L25ObTBgTJA

[2] https://firstround.com/review/the-three-tools-netflix-used-to-build-its-world-class-brand/

[3] www.aerogrammestudio.com/2013/06/05/back-to-the-story-spine/

[4] https://resources.kenblanchard.com/blanchard-leaderchat/developing-your-leadership-point-of-view

[5] For more info about Noel Tichy's work, take a look at this video: www.youtube.com/watch?v=Jfti0_vxO0c

[6] https://resources.blanchard.com/leadership-skills/developing-your-leadership-point-of-view

Chapter 8: Story finding

[1] www.dysoninstitute.ac.uk/about-us/who-we-are/our-story/

[2] www.3m.com/3M/en_US/company-us/about-3m/history/

[3] https://hbr.org/2012/12/your-companys-history-as-a-leadership-tool

[4] www.researchgate.net/publication/242134725_Using_history_in_organizations_How_managers_make_purposeful_reference_to_history_in_strategy_processes

[5] www.yiannisgabriel.com/2021/02/anchored-in-past-identities-and.html

[6] www.youtube.com/watch?v=yHyLiVrM-J8

Chapter 9: Story making

[1] www.anecdote.com/2021/09/why-communication-fails-being-abstract/

Chapter 10: Story performing

[1] www.feldsparconsulting.com/change-stories/

[2] www.anecdote.com/2018/09/what-makes-a-compelling-story/

[3] www.stevedenning.com/documents/storytellinginhbrdec07.pdf

[4] www.ideasonstage.com/ultimate-public-speaking-guide/

[5] www.presentationzen.com

[6] https://medium.com/swlh/data-storytelling-how-can-numbers-tell-tales-47c760ea5129

[7] https://pelinturgut.com/storytelling/what-happens-when-we-sit-in-circles/

[8] https://see.oregonstate.edu/sites/see.oregonstate.edu/files/story_circles_toolkit_osu_august_2020.pdf

Chapter 11: Story honing

[1] www.ted.com/talks/andrew_stanton_the_clues_to_a_great_story?language=en

Index